The
WISHING TREE

The
WISHING TREE

*How to make toys, gifts and nature crafts from leaves,
flowers, twigs, cones, seeds, shells, feathers, sand, fruit
and vegetables, eggs, paper and cardboard and more*

Pamela Allardice

Hodder & Stoughton

Every effort has been made to trace and
acknowledge copy material, but this has not always
been possible. The publishers and editors would be pleased
to hear from any copyright holders who
have not been acknowledged.

Editor: Elizabeth Neate
Designer: Anna Soo
Cover Design: Liz Seymour
Illustrations: Sue Ninham
Editorial Assistant: Ella Martin

A Hodder & Stoughton Book
Published in Australia in 1995
by Hodder Headline Australia Pty Limited,
(a member of the Hodder Headline Group)
10–16 South Street, Rydalmere NSW 2116

National Library of Australia Cataloguing-in-
Publication data

Allardice, Pamela, 1958-
The wishing tree: and other toys, games and nature
crafts for children

ISBN 0 7336 0103 0

1. Nature craft. 2. Toy making. I. Title
745.5

Printed in Australia

DEDICATION

To my mother

Know you what it is to be a child?

It is to believe in love, to believe in loveliness,

to believe in belief;

it is to be so little that the elves can reach to whisper in your ear;

it is to turn pumpkins into coaches, and mice into horses,

lowness into loftiness, and nothing into everything,

for each child has its fairy godmother in its own soul.

Percy Bysshe Shelley (1792–1822)

CONTENTS

THE WISHING TREE

The Wishing Tree is all about finding things to 'make and do' that give children an appreciation of nature and of the joys inherent in 'found' treasures like sand, stones, rocks, flowers, twigs and feathers. There are also plenty of suggestions for great 'recycled' toys, like finger puppets and wild-beast masks, which can be easily made from that bit of so-called rubbish you were going to throw out, such as an egg carton or cereal packet.

I got the idea for writing this book after a particularly wet and vexing weekend with my two boys, when I had succumbed to driving to the local toy emporium to part with hard-earned cash for more pieces of gimcrack plastic. As a rule, I like tinkering about in toy shops and don't mind fun parlours on occasion. This time, however, I came home feeling more than usually unsettled by the shopping trip. I felt as though we had somehow been conned into temporary 'fun' by buying a toy that would have to be replaced in a very short space of time by another, and then another ...

Also, the process of shopping in the toy emporium, of being guided to the appropriate aisle by robots and robotic assistants, and of being bombarded with electronic messages, price codes and flashing signs, might have been futuristic but it did not fit my ideas of what fun for kids should be. When I came across a child-sized model of a very expensive European car — at a price tag that would have kept our family in groceries for a month! — I decided it was time we came home.

I made tea while the boys settled down to inspect their new possessions. I just could not shake off my black mood and, after a bit, I realised that I wasn't just irritated by the rain and the children's general rattiness. Something deep in my core had been rocked by our trip to this particular shop, and I felt very worried about the messages that my kids were getting. I started to think about the kind of childhood I had had. More leisurely than today, certainly, but also richer and more complex. And, as I looked out at the rain streaming down the windows, I remembered my mother teaching me how to make ink from berries, and how to thread popcorn necklaces. I remembered making leaf prints and watching snail races and making a puppet show out of wooden spoons dressed in tea-towels behind the old wooden clothes horse on Nanna's verandah. (I must add that I also remembered playing with my Barbies and loving that, too — the point being that I remembered enjoying both types of toys equally.)

I know that not everyone has been lucky enough to have a childhood like mine. To some it would seem impossibly idyllic. To others it might seem boring or unimportant to want to write a book about making mushroom prints and pebble monsters. But this book is for all those parents or carers who might have had the same niggling doubts that I had after that rainy afternoon at the toy emporium. Parents who, without wishing to shield their children from the wonders of the 21st century, nonetheless hope that they will retain some respect for and knowledge of those simple, funny, affordable and enjoyable childhood pursuits that have served the human race well for many hundreds of years.

Perhaps The Lesson of the Rainy Day at the Toy Emporium boils down to this: bringing up children in our rapidly changing world is about balance and choice. It's about ensuring that they receive a balanced view of the world and its many products and services and it's about the responsibility that a parent or carer has in choosing what sorts of toys children are exposed to, and how often, at least during these first years. After that, you can only hope that they will choose to take on information and entertainment from both worlds, as it were — enjoying the amazing present and future, but also honouring the past and all it has to offer.

Most of my friends who have children are in the same boat as my husband, Greg, and I. We're all working hard to ensure that our children have chances, that they have a good education and nice clothes and all the rest of it. But when was the last time you actually wasted time together, dawdled along a muddy path and picked up sticks and then made something with them? Or stuck 'collected' pebbles or dried grasses in a jar? I'd like to think that *The Wishing Tree* provides plenty of ideas for yarning, daydreaming, shooting the breeze, cloud-watching and otherwise just plain 'wasting time' with your kids.

Most of the ideas in the book are just that — ideas that you

can suggest to children, to help them start a project off, like threading berries or flowers into chains. You can then leave them to develop the fun further themselves. There are more of these sorts of ideas than there are planned craft projects. I think that children crave variety and doing lots of little things tends to be more appealing than tackling one great big project, particularly for the littlies. Also, the thought that I had in my mind while writing *The Wishing Tree* was to include plenty of things that the children can do themselves so that they can say 'I made it myself', rather than having had to follow instructions.

Before you write me off as a hopeless romantic, or think that I have perfect children who go along with all of Mum's ideas, let me assure you that they don't and that we are a normal family. By which I mean that we fight, we get tired, we laugh, cry (a lot) and eat (well, I'm still convinced that my son Randall lives on air). Our children are a bottomless pit when it comes to requiring information and entertainment — our house resounds to 'Why?' 'When?' and 'How?' every waking hour, so I am the first to realise how tempting it is to buy something — anything — just to shut them up. My kids go to birthday parties, eat far too many sweets, get overexcited, watch TV, go on trains, swim, watch videos, and, respectively, go to playgroup and the best public school in the world. We worry about them but we don't wrap them in cottonwool and we are always honest with them. In short, Greg and I have tried to have a balanced approach to bringing them up — and some days are better than others!

Life is unpredictable. We are all busy, all the time, and I know how easy it is to slip into a position where you are suddenly too busy for each other. Scary. And unhealthy. As a 'parent in the trenches', I hope that *The Wishing Tree* reaches out to other parents and carers who value spending time with their children. I know that some of the ideas here are hard to reconcile with the busyness of our modern materialistic society. Doing nothing. Pottering around the garden. Lying down and

watching the sunset. Brunch. Sitting down and making something. But these things are not silly or romantic — they are essential to our health and happiness.

I wrote *The Wishing Tree* at the kitchen sink, literally. Edward might have said something or picked up something to show me or asked a question and the project or answer that it prompted has made up a section in the book. I suggest that the best way to use the book is for you to scan it for ideas that appeal to you, that are appropriate to where you live, for instance, or to a particular interest your child might have at the moment. None of the projects are difficult, nor do they usually require very much time and money. Bounce a few ideas off the kids — 'How about you and I make a mermaid headband for you to wear to the fancy dress party next week? If we go down to the beach on Saturday, you can choose the shells'.

The simplest, most prosaic thing can trigger a wonderful project for you both. 'Don't throw out your apple pips — I'll show you how to grow a tree.' Some 'natural' toy ideas can even become new family traditions — my friend Suzanne always gets her children to help with colouring eggs at Easter, for instance. Or you could make wonderful messy wreaths of autumn leaves that drop all over the place (but don't worry about it), and teach the children about the beauty in the changing seasons. As I get older, I truly believe that a sense of continuity, via activities like these, is one of the most valuable gifts we can give our children.

And, if you're having the day I had yesterday, when I felt I was stretched to breaking point and was completely unequal to the task of being a mother — let alone spending time with my kids making toys — take a minute to go look out the window at the clouds. It's amazing how this makes things look better.

Love, *Aurela Alladina*

So, how to start?

Almost without realising I was doing it, I have set up 'useful boxes' around the house for the boys to put things in that 'might come in handy'. Cones, the ubiquitous egg cartons, hollow beads, small jars, feathers, bits of old stockings or dresses, ice-block sticks, matchboxes, rubber bands, paperclips, interestingly shaped rocks, odd bits of bark that look like faces, and seed pods. I now buy sticky tape in 12-roll packs and industrial-sized jars of craft glue. I never run out of felt-tip pens, paintbrushes, crayons, staplers and masking tape if I can help it, and I have a secret cache of yet more sticky tape in the cellar, just in case. Edward's godmother, my good friend Amanda, keeps us supplied with reams of old office paper and bits of scrap cardboard. When the boys have finally finished with what they've made, we mulch it for the garden. I keep an eye out for recyclable treasures like buttons, wire, string and hinges, and bring them back to fight another day in the 'useful boxes'.

Important Note

Most of the projects in this book are for very simple things that a child or children can do by themselves. Some require adult supervision or help with the use of things like knives or a stove but, in the main, they are more likely to be messy than dangerous. Be sure to spread out plenty of newspaper before embarking on any project involving dried leaves or flowers, or paint!

Let common sense be your guide when exploring the world of 'natural' toys. Keep a careful eye on what berries or flowers children collect, for instance — make sure they know never to put anything in their mouths. It's also a good idea to keep essential oils, which are used in the potpourri and sachet recipes, well out of reach of babies and toddlers, as they are poisonous.

KEY

The projects in *The Wishing Tree* are for children of all ages and stages. They are graded to give you some idea of difficulty and whether or not parental supervision or guidance will be necessary.

Simple projects that children can have fun doing on their own or with friends. Young children, however, may need help from an adult to get started.

More complicated projects that children will enjoy with a little help from an adult.

These projects require adult supervision and guidance for safety's sake and for best results.

Chapter One
THINGS YOU FIND

When you next go for a walk, keep your eyes peeled. Even if you live in a city — as we do — you are still likely to find stones, feathers, twigs or interesting leaves and flowers. Even bits of so-called rubbish, like corks or cardboard lids and paper bags, might all come in handy to make something. When my husband, Greg, takes our sons out walking, they always take two bags: one is for nice interesting things that they can use at home, while the other is for real rubbish, like old bottles and chip packets, which selfish people have dropped. (This second bag goes in the garbage — or the recycling bin — when they get home, making that walk nicer for whoever goes on it next time.)

LEAVES

Leaves mark the changing of the seasons — lovely soft new green leaves in spring, thick and glossy overhead in summer, and changing to rich gold and red in autumn before falling in winter. Leaves come in many different shapes, sizes and colours, and make wonderfully interesting, one-of-a-kind playthings and project materials. Encourage children to look closely at leaves. Show them the different textures and patterns and how beautiful they are.

Leaf Light Catcher

Make this light catcher and hang it in your window. Watch the sunlight as it comes through the leaves and flowers, changing their colours.

INGREDIENTS
clear self-adhesive plastic film
small dried leaves and flowers, in a variety
of shapes and colours
cord or ribbon

EQUIPMENT
scissors
hole punch

Cut out two circles from the plastic film, each approximately 12.5cm (5in) in diameter. Peel the backing paper from one of these and place it, sticky side up, on the work surface.

On a separate piece of paper, work out how you want to arrange the dried leaves and flowers. Remember that when you place them on the sticky film they will stay there! Pick up the leaves and flowers and place them on the adhesive surface in a pattern or design.

Peel backing paper from the other circle and press this, sticky side down, over the leaves and flowers. Trim edge.

I think that I shall never see

A poem lovely as a tree ...

A tree that looks at God all day,

And lifts her leafy arms to pray;

A tree that may in summer wear

A nest of robins in her hair ...

Poems are made by fools like me,

But only God can make a tree.

JOYCE KILMER, 'TREES' (1914)

Leaf Light Catcher

Make a hole in the top of the light catcher with the hole punch, and hang it in a window with the ribbon or cord so that the light shines through the coloured leaves and flowers.

One good way of seeing just how different leaves are is to use different ones for printing, as stencils, and in wax rubbings and collages — this way, you can see the patterns in detail, and appreciate the shapes.

Leaf Printing

Once you've got the hang of leaf printing, it is a quick and easy way to decorate a whole set of envelopes and notepaper or cards as a gift, or to make bookmarks as presents.

INGREDIENTS
butcher's paper
selection of fresh leaves (ones with thick veins or ribs and markings are best)
poster paints
EQUIPMENT
newspaper
paint roller
rag or old tea-towel

Spread out some newspaper and place a piece of butcher's paper on top. Place the leaves on another sheet of newspaper.

Using the paint roller apply a thickish coat of paint to one side of a leaf, making sure you cover it evenly. Now place it face down on the butcher's paper. Place the rag or tea-towel over the leaf and press down evenly and gently.

Take away the rag and slowly peel off the leaf to see what pattern it has left.

Variation: You can make a very attractive picture by using different shades of paint and different-shaped leaves, overlapping one after the other. Framed, this leaf print picture makes a great present.

Leaf Stencilling

INGREDIENTS
selection of fresh leaves that have interesting, strong shapes, e.g. maple, oak, fern
white drawing paper
poster paints
EQUIPMENT
newspaper
reusable adhesive, e.g. Blu-Tack
saucer
sponge

Spread out newspaper as this is a messy project. Place the leaf or leaves on white paper in a shape or pattern that pleases you, and use small pinches of the reusable adhesive to hold it in place.

Put some poster paint in the saucer. Dip the sponge lightly into the poster paint, making sure that there is an even coating on the sponge's surface. Paint should not be 'taken up' by the sponge, or it will not create the patterned effect you're after.

Dab the sponge around the edges of the leaf pattern, making sure you don't leave any edges that have not been marked. Peel off leaf and you will have a stencilled design.

Variation: Experiment with moving the sponge in different ways once you have got the hang of this technique. With each dab, you could give a little twist in one direction — this makes a comma-like effect. Another idea is to use different colours. First, lightly sponge an outline with one colour, then dab another colour over the top, creating a two-tone effect.

Leaf Rubbings

You will have plenty of fun making lots of different leaf rubbings. One good idea is to use large pieces of butcher's paper or art paper — this way you can make really unusual wrapping paper for a gift.

INGREDIENTS
selection of different leaves (those with contrasting shapes, sizes and ribbing patterns will be best)
large sheets of plain white or pale-coloured art paper
thick wax crayons
EQUIPMENT
rough drawing paper
reusable adhesive, e.g. Blu-Tack, or modelling clay
sticky tape

Arrange the leaves in a pattern on the rough drawing paper; and stick them firmly in place with a small flat piece of reusable adhesive or modelling clay. Place the sheet of white or coloured art paper over the top and use sticky tape to secure it lightly around the edges.

Rock-a-bye, baby, on the tree top

When the wind blows,

the cradle will rock;

When the bough breaks,

the cradle will fall,

And down will come baby,

cradle and all.

Run a wax crayon lightly over the top of the paper from side to side, covering the whole piece of paper, so that the leaves' shapes come through as rubbings — use different colours, if you like.

Gently peel off the sticky tape from around the edges.

Wax Leaf Necklaces

These necklaces are very special because each one is unique, like the leaves. Try making a matching wreath or belt and using the set for fairy dress-ups.

INGREDIENTS

red or green wax candle
white art paper
selection of different leaves
(firm ones with heavy ribbing are best)
thread or shirring elastic
white cardboard

EQUIPMENT

spoon
scissors

Rub the candle all over one side of a sheet of white paper until it has a thick wax coating.

Place the leaves ribbed side uppermost on a flat smooth surface. Put the white paper over them, with the waxy side down. Pressing down evenly and gently so that the paper and leaves don't slip, rub the back of the waxed paper with the rounded bowl of a spoon. Rub firmly and quickly and with some pressure. Lift away the waxed sheet and on the waxy side you should see an exact transfer of the leaves you have been copying.

Cut around the leaves, leaving a narrow rim around them, and either thread on shirring elastic or thread, or mount on a strip of cardboard as a choker.

Nature Walk Collage

For best results with your collage, choose things that are flattish and have interesting textures or patterns, like bark and leaves, rather than rounded or smooth things.

INGREDIENTS
**selection of seeds, leaves, pieces of bark, stones, shells, twigs, dried fern
2 pieces of white art paper
craft glue
coloured wax crayons**
EQUIPMENT
sticky tape

Arrange your selection of items on one piece of paper, and glue in place. When the glue is dry, tape the other piece of paper over the top. Rub the wax crayons gently over the top to make a rubbing of your collage.

Foil Plaque

INGREDIENTS
**selection of round, smooth and raised objects, such as bark and pebbles
paper
craft glue
kitchen foil**

Make a collage, as above, but instead of putting another sheet of paper over the top, take a large sheet of kitchen foil and press the foil gently onto and around the objects. Take care not to puncture or tear the foil.

Leaf Wreath

INGREDIENTS
**250g (8oz) paraffin wax
small oval-shaped leaves with
stems, e.g. gum or bay
thread**
EQUIPMENT
**double boiler
fine-mesh baking rack
greaseproof paper
needle**

Melt the paraffin wax in the double boiler over gently simmering water. Holding the leaves by their stems, dip them one at a time into the wax until each leaf is completely covered, then lift out and place on the rack covered with greaseproof paper to dry.

When the wax leaves are firm, but still very slightly warm to the touch, thread the needle and sew the leaves together, overlapping one over the other to form a wreath. Finish by passing the thread through the first leaf and knotting to secure.

Fern Candles

INGREDIENTS
**350g (11oz) paraffin wax
35g (1oz) stearin
essential oil (optional)
dried fern leaves
vegetable oil**
EQUIPMENT
**candle moulds and wicks
(from craft shop)
double boiler
old saucepan
paintbrush
cottonwool**

Prepare the moulds and insert the wicks following the manufacturer's instructions. (There are usually six or 12 moulds in a set, depending on the size and shape of candle you want.)

Melt the wax in the top half of the double boiler over simmering water. Melt the stearin in the old saucepan, then add it to the wax. Also add the essential oil now if you wish to include it. Stir well. Pour the wax into the moulds and allow it to set. Keep a little of the wax aside for attaching the fern leaves.

When the candles are firm, trim the wicks. Remelt the reserved wax, paint it on the back of the fern leaves and press them firmly onto the candles. Leave to harden. Brush lightly over the top of the fern leaves with the last of the wax to secure. To give the candles a smooth finish, polish them with cottonwool dipped into vegetable oil.

Leaf Skeletons

INGREDIENTS
**selection of different types of leaves
(collect big and small, thick and thin ones)
sheet of art paper
craft glue**
EQUIPMENT
**large saucepan
washing soda
newspaper
soft toothbrush
plastic ice-cream container
1 tablespoon bleach
sieve**

Half-fill the saucepan with water, add a handful of washing soda and bring to a simmer. Drop the leaves into the water, reduce the heat to low and simmer for 45 minutes, or until the fleshy part of the leaves has come away, leaving behind the skeletons.

Strain off the leaf skeletons and spread them out on newspaper. Brush very gently with the toothbrush to get rid of any remaining fleshy parts.

Half-fill the ice-cream container with cold water and add a tablespoon of bleach; mix well until thoroughly dissolved. Put the leaf skeletons into this mixture and leave for a further 45 minutes.

Gently strain the skeletons, using a sieve, and then rinse them very gently under slow-running cold water.

Why not arrange your leaf skeletons in a pattern on a piece of paper to display them? Use a dab of glue to fix them in place.

Glycerine Leaves

INGREDIENTS
branch of leaves from evergreen plants (such as ivy) or deciduous trees (such as maple and oak)
glycerine
EQUIPMENT
large jar
soft cloth or rag

Fill a jar with a mixture of 1 part glycerine and 2 parts hot water.

Remove any discoloured leaves from the branch and slit the base of the stem about 1.5cm ($\frac{1}{2}$in) from the bottom. With harder ends of, say, small branches, you need to hammer them gently about 6.5cm ($2\frac{1}{2}$in) up the stem.

Stand the stems in the glycerine mixture. Inspect the leaves frequently to make sure they do not become oversaturated. When liquid begins to ooze out of the surface of the leaves, remove them, wipe them with the soft cloth or rag, and hang to dry in a warm, airy place.

When the leaves are dry, stand the branch in a vase or tall bottle. The leaves will last for months and gradually turn different colours.

If you are giving a friend or relative a book as a present, you might like to add a bookmark that you have made yourself. Or you could include an original gift tag. You will notice that some of these projects use pressed or dried leaves. You can find out how to press flowers and leaves on page 21, and how to dry them on page 15.

Four-leaf Clover Bookmark

INGREDIENTS
stiff art or construction paper, in your choice of colour
pressed clover leaves (preferably four-leaf, but several of the three-leaf kind will do!)
craft glue
EQUIPMENT
pencil
ruler
scissors
small, soft, fine-tipped paintbrush
tweezers

Use the pencil, ruler and scissors to measure and cut a strip of the coloured paper 4 x 18cm ($1\frac{1}{2}$ x 7in).

Pick up the dried clover leaves with the tweezers and use the paintbrush to paint the back of the leaves carefully with the glue. Place four of them together on one end of the paper strip. Set aside and allow to dry thoroughly before use.

Rosemary Bookmark

INGREDIENTS
**stiff parchment paper, in your choice of
colour
sprigs of pressed rosemary
craft glue
clear self-adhesive plastic film, 25 x 30cm
(10 x 12in)
bias binding or grosgrain ribbon in
colour matching parchment paper, 45cm
(18in) long
ribbon or silk cord, 1cm (³/₈in) wide and
30cm (12in) long**
EQUIPMENT
**pencil
ruler
scissors
tweezers
small, soft, fine-tipped paintbrush**

Use the pencil, ruler and scissors to measure and cut a strip of the parchment paper 4 x 18cm (1½ x 7in).

Pick up the pressed rosemary sprigs with the tweezers and use the paintbrush to paint the back of the sprigs with the glue. Arrange them on the bookmark. Cover the bookmark with the plastic film and trim to fit.

Finish by gluing bias binding or grosgrain ribbon around the bookmark's edges, folding and turning in extra fabric at the corners. Glue the length of ribbon or silk cord to the top, or punch a hole through the top of the bookmark and thread the ribbon or cord through.

Leaf Gift Tags

INGREDIENTS
**paper or light card
narrow ribbon, in colour matching paper
or card
craft glue
dried or pressed flowers**
EQUIPMENT
pinking shears

Cut the paper or card in a leaf shape with the pinking shears, and glue on a ribbon loop. Add a personal touch by gluing on some dried or pressed flowers.

Variation: Another great idea is to use the dried leaves and petals themselves as tags. Large maple or gum leaves and fully blown rose petals may be pressed until the sap has gone and they are crisp, like paper. Write your message using dark grey or green ink and a mapping pen, pressing very carefully so as not to crack the leaf or petal.

Jewel Grass

INGREDIENTS
**red, green and yellow food dyes
dried grasses (the best grasses to use are
those with fluffy heads)**
EQUIPMENT
**newspaper
rubber gloves
old plastic containers**

(ice-cream containers are perfect)
3 or 4 sticks, or old knitting needles
butcher's paper
bottle or jug

Spread out the newspaper and put on the rubber gloves. Place the plastic containers on the newspaper.

Mix the food dyes separately, and pour one colour into each of the three containers to a depth of about 4cm (1½ in).

Place some of the grasses in each of the containers, using the sticks or knitting needles to keep them fully immersed in the dye.

Take the grasses out and lay them, one at a time, on the butcher's paper until most of the water is absorbed. Then stand them in the bottle or jug to dry in a warm, airy place. If the fluffy heads have clumped up after their dye bath, use a hair dryer to fluff them up again.

Tablemats and Coasters

INGREDIENTS
thin cardboard
thin cork board or matting
dried leaves
craft glue
clear self-adhesive plastic film
EQUIPMENT
pencil
ruler
scissors
scrap paper

Cut out four pieces of cardboard 25 x 30cm (10 x 12in) for the tablemats, and four pieces 7.5cm (3in) square for the coasters. Cut out eight pieces of thin cork board or matting the same size as the pieces of cardboard.

On a piece of scrap paper, arrange the leaves in the design you would like — perhaps you could make four daisy-chain shapes on the mats and matching smaller ones for the coasters. Initials and wavy border designs can look good too.

When you are happy with the design, pick up each leaf and apply a few dabs of glue to the back, then glue to the pieces of cardboard.

When the glue is dry, mount cardboard onto the pieces of cork board or matting.

Then cut four large and four small pieces of the plastic film, each about 1.5cm ($\frac{1}{2}$in) bigger all around than the tablemat or coaster. Cover the front of each tablemat and coaster with plastic film, folding the edges to the back.

Leaf Lampshade

INGREDIENTS
brown wrapping paper
purchased cylindrical lampshade frame
thin cardboard
craft glue
selection of different fresh, flat leaves
clear self-adhesive plastic film
masking tape
EQUIPMENT
scissors
stapler

Cut a rectangle from the brown paper, which will wrap around the lampshade frame, allowing for a 2.5cm (1in) overlap at the sides and a 1.5cm (1/2in) overlap top and bottom. Wrap a piece of cardboard around the lampshade frame and cut to fit exactly. Position the cardboard in the centre of the paper, leaving the edges free, and glue. Arrange the leaves on the paper, leaving the edges free.

Leaf Lampshade

Cut a piece of plastic film, 1.5cm (½in) wider than the work all around and press down evenly over the leaves, squeezing out any air bubbles; this will help to preserve the leaves. Turn in the top and bottom overlaps, using the 1.5cm (½in) strips of plastic film to secure evenly, top and bottom.

Curve the cardboard into a cylinder shape and wrap it around the lampshade frame, overlapping the ends. The clear plastic strip should be reinforced with masking tape or staples.

Leaf Card Game

INGREDIENTS
12 pairs of matching leaves (small enough to fit on playing cards, but different shapes, e.g. gum, Japanese maple, rose, fern)
poster paints
12 sheets of butcher's paper
2 large sheets of thick white cardboard, cut into 24 playing card pieces, each approx. 5 x 10cm (2 x 4in)
craft glue

EQUIPMENT
newspaper
paintbrush
scissors

Spread out the newspaper. Take the first pair of leaves and paint the underside (ribbed side) with poster paint. One at a time, press the leaves carefully onto butcher's paper, rubbing gently over the back to get an even print.

You may need to repeat this several times until you have two prints on that piece of butcher's paper that are very nearly the same. Put that piece of butcher's paper aside to dry. Repeat the process with the other pairs of leaves, until you have two good matching prints of each.

When all the leaf prints are dry, cut out the two best of each kind and glue one onto each playing card. Allow to dry.

To play the game, mix up all the pairs of cards and lay them face down on the table. Taking turns, each player turns over two cards. If the cards match, they take those cards away; if they don't, they put them back face down on the table. The winner is the person with the most pairs when the game is finished.

FLOWERS

The best thing about flowers is their smell. Three favourites, all easy to grow and with beautiful scents, are mignonette, bergamot and lavender. It is easy to learn how to make a scented tea by adding a few bergamot leaves to the pot, and to scatter dried lavender in the linen press to make sheets and towels smell nice. Mignonette, picked and put in a vase in the kitchen or on the dining-room table, will perfume a whole room.

Lavender Wand

INGREDIENTS
**30 fresh lavender flowers, on stalks as long as possible
narrow pink or mauve satin ribbon, 90cm (3ft) long**

Using the ribbon, tie the lavender flowers together firmly, just beneath where the stem starts. Bend each of the stems back gently below the ribbon so that they form a 'cage' over the flowers, and then tie the bottom of the stems together.

Weave the long ends of the ribbon over and under the stems, moving down the wand until all the lavender is enclosed. Stitch the ribbon ends together firmly, and finish with a bow.

Potpourri is a lovely traditional way to fill a room with the scent of flowers all year round. The finished effect can be beautiful, too, particularly if you choose flowers and leaves with interesting shapes and colours to dry.

Note for the grown-ups: Making potpourri may require a little bit of help. It's also a good idea to always keep essential oils well out of reach of smaller children and to explain to older ones that, even though the oils smell lovely, they should never be tasted because they are poisonous.

Ring a ring o' roses

A pocket full of posies

Atishoo, atishoo,

We all fall down.

Lavender's blue, dilly dilly,

Lavender's green

When I am king, dilly dilly,

You'll be my queen.

Spicy Lemon Potpourri

INGREDIENTS
1 tablespoon dried lemon verbena leaves
1 tablespoon dried lemon balm leaves
1 tablespoon dried lemon thyme leaves
3 dried bay leaves, crumbled
1 tablespoon dried lemon zest
1 teaspoon dried orange zest
few drops neroli oil
few drops orange essential oil
2 tablespoons dried marigold petals or
small yellow everlasting daisies
EQUIPMENT
large china or glazed ceramic bowl
eye-dropper
pretty glass or china bowl

Place the dried leaves and zest in the china or glazed ceramic bowl and mix well with your hands. Add the essential oils, a drop at a time, until the desired level of fragrance is reached.

Drying Flowers for Potpourri

Collect leaves and flowers that you want to dry in the early morning — this way they are more likely to retain their colours. Spread them out on a tray and put them in a warm, airy place. They'll be ready in a few weeks. You can also use pressed flowers in your potpourri.

Pour into the pretty glass or china bowl and decorate the top with the dried marigold petals or everlasting daisies.

Fruit and Cinnamon Potpourri

INGREDIENTS
1 orange, thinly sliced
2 tablespoons cloves
1 lemon, thinly sliced and quartered
1 apple, thinly sliced and halved
2 cinnamon sticks, broken into 2.5cm
(1in) pieces
4 tablespoons dried peppermint leaves
1 tablespoon dried orange zest
1 tablespoon dried lemon zest
1 tablespoon orris root powder (from the
chemist)
few drops essential oil of orange or
lemon
EQUIPMENT
fine-mesh baking rack
large china or glazed ceramic bowl
eye-dropper
pretty glass or china bowl

Stud the peel of the orange slices with cloves. Spread out the orange, lemon and apple slices on a fine-mesh baking rack, and dry in a very slow oven for several hours until quite leathery to the touch. It is important that the fruit is quite dry, for if it is still moist it will cause the potpourri to go mouldy.

Place the cinnamon sticks, peppermint leaves, dried apple and lemon pieces, zest and orris root powder in the china or glazed ceramic bowl and mix well with your hands. Add a few drops of essential oil, a drop at a time, until the desired level of fragrance is reached.

Place the potpourri in the glass or china bowl and decorate the top with the dried clove-studded orange slices.

Fairy's Potpourri

INGREDIENTS
2 tablespoons dried dark red or pink rose petals
2 tablespoons dried violets
1 tablespoon dried blue cornflowers
1 tablespoon dried lemon-scented geranium leaves
1 tablespoon dried lavender
1 teaspoon cloves, crushed
cinnamon stick, broken into small pieces
1/2 teaspoon allspice powder
1 tablespoon orris root powder (from the chemist)
few drops rose and violet essential oils
10–12 dried purple and yellow pansies

EQUIPMENT
large china or glazed ceramic bowl
eye-dropper
pretty glass bowl
opened-out hairpin or piece of wire

Place the rose petals, violets, cornflowers, geranium leaves and lavender in the china or glazed ceramic bowl with the crushed cloves and cinnamon stick pieces.

Mix together the allspice powder and orris root powder and sprinkle over the flower mixture. Mix all the ingredients together well with your hands. Add the essential oil, a drop at a time, until the desired level of fragrance is reached.

The nicest way to display this potpourri is in a glass bowl. Slide all except two of the dried purple and yellow pansies down the sides, using the opened-out hairpin or piece of wire to position them. Place the remaining pansies on top of the potpourri.

Potpourri Card

INGREDIENTS
thin cardboard
scraps of lace or thin material, such as lawn
potpourri mix
craft glue
extra scraps of lace or felt-tip pens

EQUIPMENT
pencil
ruler
scissors

Cut out your card from the cardboard, approximately 25cm (10in) square, and fold it in half. Sketch a circle or heart shape on the front of the card and cut it out carefully.

Measure enough lace or material to make a sachet that will be slightly larger all

round than the cut-out shape. Stitch the sides of the sachet together, leaving a narrow opening. Fill loosely with a spoonful or so of potpourri mix — no more, or the card will be too chunky — and stitch the opening together.

Run a thin line of glue around the cut-out shape on the inside of the card and press the sachet's edges firmly onto it. Put a light weight on top and leave to dry.

Finish the card by decorating the edges with the extra scraps of lace, or use the felt-tip pens to draw pictures of the flowers and herbs that are in the potpourri mix.

Perfumed Sachet

The easiest way to make a sachet is to use two pretty lace-edged handkerchiefs. That way, most of the work is already done and you can make the sachet in a very short time.

To make sachet mix

INGREDIENTS
1 cup dried dark red or pink scented rose petals
1 tablespoon dried elderflowers
1 tablespoon dried lavender flowers
2 tablespoons dried rosemary leaves
1 tablespoon dried grated orange zest
1 tablespoon orris root powder (from the chemist)
few drops neroli or rose essential oil
EQUIPMENT
large china or glazed ceramic bowl
eye-dropper

Place the petals, flowers, leaves and zest in a large china or glazed ceramic bowl and mix well with your hands. Add the orris root powder and mix it in, and then add the essential oil, a drop at a time, until the desired level of fragrance is reached.

When the first baby laughed for the first time, the laugh broke into a thousand pieces and they all went skipping about, and that was the beginning of fairies.

SIR J. M. BARRIE, *PETER PAN* (1928)

To make sachet

INGREDIENTS
plain white muslin, 50cm (20in) long
white thread
2 lace-edged handkerchiefs
ribbon bow or appliqué flower
EQUIPMENT
scissors
needle

Cut two squares of muslin about 15 x 18cm (6 x 7in) and machine or hand sew around three of the four sides. Turn right side out and fill with several spoonfuls of the sachet mix, then stitch up the fourth seam by hand.

Place the lace-edged handkerchiefs with right sides together and lace trim tucked into the centre, and machine or hand sew around three of the four sides. Turn right side out and insert the muslin sachet. Close the handkerchief sachet, using small slip stitches between the two sections of lace trim.

Decorate the front of the sachet with a ribbon bow or an appliqué flower.

Herbal Bath Bags

Herbs and flowers smell beautiful in a bath but rather than putting them directly into the tub, where they will stick to your skin and clog up the plug hole, it is better to put spoonfuls of the mixture into bath bags and add these to the bath as the water is running. Bath bags make wonderful made-it-myself presents for relatives and friends, too. You can pick and dry the herbs and flowers yourself, or buy them very cheaply from florists, nurseries or garden supply shops. Adding a few drops of essential oil will make the mixture smell even lovelier. If the bags are to be a gift, put a little card with them explaining how they are used.

INGREDIENTS
2 tablespoons dried chamomile flowers
2 tablespoons dried mint leaves
2 tablespoons dried lemon balm leaves
1 tablespoon pine needles
1 tablespoon rosemary leaves
2 tablespoons bran
4 pretty towelling face cloths
4 lengths of ribbon
EQUIPMENT
large china or glazed ceramic bowl

Mix together the flowers, leaves, pine needles and bran in the bowl, using your hands to ensure they are well blended.

Spread out the face cloths and divide the mixture evenly between them, placing the mixture in a heap in the centre of each face cloth. Gather up the sides to make a pouch and tie firmly with a length of the ribbon.

Wet the bag in the bath and use it as a sponge. The water will release the milky bran essence and beautiful natural perfumes into the water.

Perfumed Notepaper

INGREDIENTS
4–6 drops favourite essential oil (such as
rose or jasmine)
2 tablespoons orris root powder
sachet bag (see p. 18)
tiny dried flowers
craft glue
box of note paper and envelopes

It is easy and fun to give notepaper a floral
perfume. Simply add the essential oil to the
orris root powder and mix together well.

Put this mixture into a sachet bag and
place it in a box, layering the sheets of
notepaper and envelopes over it, then
close the lid. Keep the lid firmly shut for
about 6 weeks.

You could also decorate the individual
sheets of notepaper with tiny dried flowers.
Just fix them into place along the top of
the sheet, or in a corner, using a dab of
glue, and allow them to dry thoroughly
before folding the paper and putting it in
an envelope.

Simple Rose Perfume

INGREDIENTS
6 tablespoons rose petals (red are best
because they have the strongest perfume)
½ cup (125ml/4fl oz) vodka

1 tablespoon fresh rosemary leaves
1 tablespoon grated orange zest
1 teaspoon grated lemon zest
2 cups (500ml/16fl oz) boiling water

EQUIPMENT
2 china or glass bowls
spoon
piece of cloth
lidded jar or bottle
sieve

Put the rose petals in a china or glass bowl
and pour the vodka over them. Stir the
mixture so that the vodka is well
distributed, and bruise the petals with the
spoon.

Cover the mixture with the piece of
cloth and store in a cool dry place for at
least 10 days. Strain off the petals with a
sieve and reserve the rose-scented liquid.

Bruise the rosemary leaves and place
with the orange and lemon zest in another
bowl. Pour boiling water over the mixture
and leave until cool; strain off the liquid.

Combine the orange liquid and the
rose-scented liquid in the lidded jar or
bottle and shake well before use. This
makes an easy and very popular gift.

There are many other traditional flower
crafts, such as drying and pressing
flowers and making flower cards, that are
enjoyable and easy to do. They might
even become a lifelong hobby!

Pussy Willow Card

INGREDIENTS
light cardboard
branches of pussy willow
felt-tip pens (optional)
craft glue
EQUIPMENT
pencil
ruler
scissors

Cut out your card from the cardboard approximately 12.5 x 15cm (5 x 6in) and fold it in half, creasing along the fold. Lightly sketch a picture on the front with the pencil — perhaps a pattern or a scene.

Pull the pussy willow buds gently off the branches. If you like, you can divide the pussy willow buds into portions and colour each portion a different colour with felt-tip pens — pink, yellow or green, for instance.

Run a thin line of glue along the sketched lines and place the pussy willow buds on the glued areas.

Pressing flowers and herbs is a very old craft. It was especially popular during the Victorian era, when young girls used pressed flowers to decorate all manner of pictures, gift cards and notepaper. Pressed flowers can also be used to decorate boxes and screens.

Pressed Flower Card

If you are good at calligraphy, you could copy out a poem (or compose your own), then illustrate it with pressed flowers. You might want to match sets of different cards to different months or seasons of the year.

INGREDIENTS
piece of stiff white art paper, 25 x 30cm (10 x 12in) (from art supply shop)
selection of pressed flowers and herbs
craft glue
EQUIPMENT
knife
clean white paper
wooden toothpicks
small, soft, fine-tipped paintbrush

Fold the art paper in half lengthwise, scoring lightly with the knife along the inside of the fold if it is too stiff to lie flat.

On a separate piece of clean white paper, set out the pressed herbs and flowers in a design of your choice — perhaps as a bouquet, or personalised with the initials of the person you will be giving the card to, or even a daisy chain (though not necessarily using daisies).

When you are satisfied with the design, start to pick up the individual pieces, and apply a very small amount of the glue with the point of a toothpick. Fix the flowers and herbs into place following your design on the front of the card, using the small, soft paintbrush to manoeuvre the pieces into place, if necessary. When the flowers are correctly positioned, press down on them with a clean piece of paper to set them in place.

Leave the glue to set properly before putting the card in an envelope.

Flower Découpage Plate

INGREDIENTS
**selection of pressed flowers and leaves,
e.g. daisies, clovers, pansies
plastic dinner plate
craft glue
purchased picture hanger
clear lacquer or varnish**
EQUIPMENT
**tweezers
fine paintbrush
wide paintbrush**

Arrange the flowers and leaves in a pattern on the plate. When you are happy with the design, pick up each piece with the tweezers and, using the fine paintbrush, cover the back with glue. Press back down in place.

When the flowers and leaves have dried completely, use the wide paintbrush to coat the entire plate with clear lacquer or varnish. Set aside to dry, then repeat with a second coat.

Attach the picture hanger to the back of the plate, either with glue or a claw attachment, and hang the plate on the wall.

Note: Do not use this plate to eat from and do not wash it, as the varnish will crack and spoil the work.

Pressing Flowers

Suitable flowers for pressing include pansies, lavender, rose petals or whole baby rosebuds and love-in-a-mist. Leaves with interesting shapes that press well are scented geraniums, sage, gum and the various mints. Herbs you might like to try pressing are borage, thyme, lemon verbena, chervil, chamomile, artemisia, dill, southern-wood, and rue.

The simplest way to start is to place small sprigs of herbs or individual flowers between sheets of clean blotting paper and then put them between the pages of a heavy book, such as the telephone directory. Place more weights on top, such as bricks or more books.

Small flower presses may be bought from craft shops and garden centres, and they make a good start for this hobby. Some of the larger ones take up to 10 layers of dried material.

Leave the herbs and flowers for 6–8 weeks before checking to see whether they are ready to use. It is important that they be quite dry, as any dampness will spoil your work.

Single petals and leaves will dry quite quickly, while flowers with thick stems or petals will take longer. If any of the flowers you choose have a thick stem or calyx — such as a jonquil or a small daffodil — split the base with a fine blade so that it presses open, otherwise it may rot rather than dry thoroughly.

Pressed Flower Picture

Suitable backing materials for a pressed flower picture include hessian or velvet, because they make a good textural contrast with the flowers. There are some very pretty, naturally dyed, recycled papers available too. Choose a plain colour that will go with the colours of the flowers you want to use, or the room where the picture will be hung. Avoid anything that is too brightly coloured, as it will make the flowers look washed-out.

INGREDIENTS

stiff art paper or material of choice, cut to fit behind purchased mount and frame
selection of pressed flowers and herbs
craft glue
aerosol fixative spray
purchased mount, frame and glass set

EQUIPMENT

pencil
clean scrap paper
tweezers
toothpicks
small, soft, fine-tipped paintbrush

Using the frame mount as a guide, trace with a pencil the area of art paper that will be seen. On a separate piece of clean paper, plan your picture.

When you are happy with the design, pick up the individual flowers and herbs with tweezers and lightly touch the back of each with the glue, using a toothpick. Move each piece into place with the tip of the small, soft paintbrush.

When you have finished arranging the flowers and herbs, take your work outside and spray with the aerosol fixative. This will invisibly seal the flowers and herbs, and protect them from moisture.

Drying Flowers

Hang bunches of leaves and flower stems upside down in the laundry or carport, or a similar area where there is a free flow of air. This works really well for ferns, roses and hydrangeas.

Leave the picture to dry thoroughly before attaching it to the mount, covering it with the glass and placing it in the frame.

When dried correctly, flowers can continue to give pleasure for many years to come. Some of these ideas, like the **Flowery Hat**, make lovely gifts for friends and relatives, who will really appreciate the thought you have put into making them.

Flowery Hat

Hats made from natural materials, such as raffia or straw, look best for this project.

INGREDIENTS
straw hat
bright-coloured ribbon or matching raffia, 2.3m (2½yd) long
selection of suitable dried flowers, such as dried whole roses, lavender heads, clove pinks, carnations, zinnias
smaller dried leaves or herbs, such as rosemary, Queen Anne's lace, star anise

EQUIPMENT
hot-glue gun

First, tie the ribbon or raffia around the crown of the hat, finishing with a large bow and streamers.

Now, choose dried flowers, leaves and herbs from your selection that tone with the ribbon to decorate the hat. Start with several of the larger flowers either in the front or the centre back, near the bow. Then arrange the rest of your selection around the sides. Use the hot-glue gun to fix the flowers, leaves and herbs in place.

Note for the grown-ups: This project involves using a hot glue gun, so adult supervision is required.

Dried Flower Arrangement

INGREDIENTS
**interesting-looking twig,
with several branches
small pot
modelling clay, or florist's oasis
pebbles or sand
different dried flowers, e.g. poppy seed
heads, gumnuts, dried beech nuts or
acorns, helichrysum flowers, sweet
honesty pods, Chinese lanterns, glycerine
leaves (see p. 9)
nuts, cones, seeds, leaves, feathery grasses
craft glue or fuse wire**

Set the twig in the pot and secure it with modelling clay. Alternatively, cut a shape from the florist's oasis to fill the base of the pot, and push the twig into that. Fill up the pot with sand or pebbles so that it will not tip over.

Glue or wire different dried flowers, leaves, and grasses, nuts, cones and seeds to the twig.

Clay Fan Vase with Dried Flowers

INGREDIENTS
**clay (available from craft shops)
dried flowers**

EQUIPMENT
**rolling pin
skewer
toothpicks
knife**

Take a large piece of clay and use the rolling pin to roll it out flat to about a 1.5cm (½in) thickness. Cut out a fan shape and score and decorate it with a skewer and/or toothpicks. Roll out another, smaller piece of clay and make a smaller fan. Score and decorate as before.

Moisten the edges of the smaller fan and press them to the base of the first one. Use your thumbs to curve it out in a vase shape and smooth the edges to secure it to the base. Use the knife to cut straight along the bottom of the joined fans to create a straight edge. Set aside to dry.

When dry, prop the vase up on its straight edge on a windowsill or mantelpiece and fill it with dried flowers.

Clay Fan Vase with Dried Flowers

Sand-drying Flowers

clean dry silver sand (from
hardware stores)
borax powder (from chemists or
hardware stores)
selection of flowers — good ones
to choose for sand-drying are
lilies, cornflowers, daffodils,
daisies, freesias, pansies,
marigolds, peonies, roses
and violets
large, flat, airtight container

Note for the grown-ups:
Borax powder is poisonous, so this
activity is probably suitable only
for older children. You will still
need to supervise this activity.

Mix together 2 parts sand with 3 parts
borax powder. Put a layer of the sand
mixture on the bottom of the airtight
container and place several flower
heads on top (daisy types face down,
others face up). Gently spoon over
more sand mixture to cover the
flowers. Tightly secure the lid.

Leave the flowers for 8–10 days,
then check. If they have dried through,
the petals should feel like tissue paper.

Unlike air-drying, the lovely thing about sand-dried flowers is that they retain their colours well.

Flower Paperweight

A flower paperweight is easy and fun to make —
it is also a very special gift for a special grown-up,
helping to keep their papers orderly on a desk or
writing table.

INGREDIENTS
scraps of green or red velvet
clear glass jar with lid (wide-necked flattish
salsa jars are ideal)
craft glue
sand-dried flowers — a large full-blown rose
the width of the neck of the jar would be
perfect — plus a few sand-dried rose leaves
reusable adhesive, e.g. Blu-Tack

Arrange the scraps of velvet on the inside of the jar lid and glue to secure. Set the sand-dried rose in the folds of the velvet with a few leaves to either side. Secure with the reusable adhesive.

Clean the glass jar so that it is quite clear with absolutely no streaks inside, up-end it over the rose and screw it into place, holding the lid firmly with the other hand so as not to disturb the flower.

Fantasy Flowers

It's easy to create 'magic' crazily coloured fantasy flowers, just for fun. They can also be used as decorations for a party room, or for 'show-and-tell' at school.

INGREDIENTS
**fresh flowers with long stems
(pale-coloured ones, like white carnations
or lilies or daffodils, are best)
food dyes
glass jars**

Place a few drops of a different-coloured food dye in each of the glass jars and top up with water. Put some of the flowers in each of the jars. Over the next day or so, the coloured water will creep up the stems of the flowers and change the colour of the flower itself.

Variation: Take a white rose and split the stem down the middle, putting one half in a glass of clear water and the other in a glass with green or blue food colouring. Half the stem will suck up the coloured water and half the plain, resulting in a zanily splotched rose.

Not only do flowers look pretty and sweet — many taste delicious too! Use them to decorate little cakes and puddings, scatter them on top of ice-cream or custard, or use the petals in cakes or blancmanges.

Crystallised Violets

I have yet to find any child who does not love to eat these! They are magical fun to make and magically delicious to nibble on.

INGREDIENTS
**violet flowers
1 or 2 egg whites, lightly whisked
caster sugar**
EQUIPMENT
**small, soft paintbrush or make-up brush
pointy-ended tweezers
greaseproof paper
fine-mesh baking rack
airtight container
absorbent paper**

Using the brush, paint the violets with the egg white holding them with the tweezers. Carefully sprinkle the flowers all over thickly with the sugar, dusting a little extra over where you have held them with the tweezers to give an even coating.

Spread the violets out on greaseproof paper, place on a fine-mesh baking rack and leave in a warm, dry place until they become brittle. Turn them occasionally so that they dry evenly.

Store the crystallised violets in an airtight container on absorbent paper for up to a week.

Edible flowers

Other pretty ideas using violets or rose petals are:

• Make flower ice cubes by putting one flower and a tiny curl of lemon rind in each compartment of an ice tray, cover with water and freeze.

• Make a wreath of flowers and place it around the edge of a bowl containing chocolate mousse.

• Experiment with making flower honeys, using lavender, rose petals, verbena leaves or mint, for instance.

Snip or crush the flower lightly, place it in a glass jar and pour warmed honey over. (Use a good-quality, organic honey for best results — commercially prepared honeys don't taste as good.)

Leave the honey in a warm sunny place for 10 days or longer, until the honey takes on the delicate taste and aroma of the flower. Strain and rebottle.

Where the bee sucks, there suck I

In a cowslip's bell I lie;

There I couch when owls do cry.

On a bat's back I do fly

After summer merrily.

Merrily, merrily shall I live now

Under the blossom that hangs on

the bough.

WILLIAM SHAKESPEARE, *THE TEMPEST* (1611)

Daisy Chains

Daisies are useful for making necklaces, anklets, crowns, belts, garlands and even skipping ropes, if you have enough. A daisy-chain crown and belt make wonderful accessories for a fairy dress-up party.

To start a chain, pick daisies with stems at least 4cm (1½ in) long. Use the very tip of your thumbnail, or else a tiny point of a nail file or butter knife, to make a narrow slit towards the end of the first stem. Make sure you do not cut all the way through to the bottom of the stem.

Slip the second daisy stem through so that the head fits snugly over the slit. Make a slit in this second stem, thread the third flower and pull it gently into place, and so on.

He loves me,

He loves me not

DRIFTWOOD, TWIGS AND CONES

One, two, buckle my shoe,

Three, four, open the door,

Five, six, pick up sticks,

Seven, eight, lay them straight,

Nine, ten, a good fat hen,

Eleven, twelve, bake it well.

As an adult, I find it quite an eye-opener to go for a walk with my children. Whereas I look around me at houses or at other people, the boys stop to pick up 'treasures' every few minutes — twigs to make slingshots, nice-shaped pieces of bark, or strange lumpy cones with 'eyes'. Then they bring them home to look at, put away for later or make something with.

Driftwood is probably the most exciting thing of all to work with. The sea has used its extraordinary power to create weird and wonderful patterns on the wood, and changed the shape of the piece in a graceful way that would probably not be seen on land.

Eye of God

This is a very old traditional ornament. Native Americans used to hang them outside their tepees to keep evil spirits away, and they also wore them as chest plates.

INGREDIENTS
2 short firm straight sticks, about 18cm (7in) long
craft glue or fuse wire
coloured yarn
beads, hollow shells or pieces of macaroni

Glue or wire the sticks together firmly to form a cross, and tie the end of the yarn to the centre of the cross.

Bring the yarn up over the right-hand arm of the cross, down and then under it. Bring the yarn behind the top arm, over and around and over again, then behind it. Bring the yarn down behind the left-hand arm of the cross, around and

Some ingredients for making Eye of God

over, then behind it. Bring the yarn behind the bottom arm of the cross, around and over, then behind it.

Repeat the procedure and continue to wrap the yarn around the cross, moving outwards along the arms, in a weaving effect. You could thread beads or pieces of macaroni onto the yarn as you get better at doing it.

To finish, glue the last 1.5cm (½in) of the last arm you wrapped and then wind three more turns around it, pressing the yarn firmly into the glue. Cut off excess.

Wishing Tree

Some time ago, a friend gave me a big piece of tortured willow. I sprayed it gold and propped it up in the corner of the room.

Then I started to hang a few favourite things on it — some old velvet flowers and a bunch of fake purple grapes, and then the Christmas fairy lights somehow stayed there, instead of being put away. When my son, Edward, started putting some of his favourite things there too, we decided to call it our wishing tree, and we all put things on it. You might want to hang family photos on your tree, pretty hair slides or favourite toys, or bags of sweets for a party, or seeds and feathers and pebbles, or other things that you find on a walk. Look for a really interestingly shaped stick, with lots of branches, for this project.

INGREDIENTS
stick with several branches, or piece of driftwood, approx. 45cm (18in) tall
spray paint
terracotta pot, 18cm (7in) diameter
modelling clay, enough to fill the terracotta pot
gloss enamel paint
decorations of choice
EQUIPMENT
newspaper

Place the stick or driftwood on newspaper and spray paint in your choice of colour; allow to dry.

Place the stick in the pot and use the modelling clay to secure it at the angle you want; firm it down thoroughly. Clip off any branches or twigs that you do not want. Fill up the pot with the rest of the modelling clay and press down firmly so that the 'tree' will not move.

Use gloss enamel paint to decorate the pot, then hang your decorations from the branches.

Fishing Pole

You need a thin stick, about 75cm (30in) long, and a piece of thin string or nylon thread. Tie one end of the string to one end of the pole and thread a fish hook to the other. Then all you need is a bait — and some good luck!

It's fun to make people from things that you have found in nature. Sometimes a piece of bark or a cone may look just like a face to start with — sometimes you can be clever and just add some 'hair' or 'eyes' and it becomes a person.

I know each lane,

and every alley green,

Dingle, or bushy dell,

of this wild wood,

And every bosky bourne from

side to side,

My daily walks and ancient

neighbourhood.

JOHN MILTON (1608–1674)

Pine Cone People

Decorate these people to make them really individual. What about little glasses made out of fuse wire, or a hat or cape made from strips of bark glued together?

INGREDIENTS
pine cones
flat pieces of thick bark for feet
craft glue
small nuts and seeds for eyes
larger nuts for noses
tufts of dried grass for hair
fuse wire
thick knobbly sticks for arms and legs

Glue pieces of bark to the bottom of the pine cones for feet so that the pine cones will stand squarely. Glue on small nuts or seeds for the eyes and a larger nut for the nose. Wire together tufts of grass and glue them on to make hair. Choose sticks for arms and legs and glue them on.

Bark or Driftwood Faces

These faces can be as mysterious or as familiar as you like. Make a normal-looking face, with eyes and nose, or make a beautiful wood fairy or magician, with leaves for hair and long twiggy fingers.

Pine cones

pieces of bark or driftwood
selection of small twigs, seeds, fir cones,
beech nuts or acorns, gumnuts, lichen
clear wood glue or craft glue
wood shavings (from a timber merchant
or pet shop)
EQUIPMENT
adjustable craft knife
sandpaper

Look at the shapes and surface textures of the bark or driftwood and pick pieces that can be shaped into a face. Ones that are curved, so that they will wrap around a face like a mask, are easiest to work with. Carve off any edges, and smooth rough sections with sandpaper.

Look at the selection of other items and see which ones suggest different parts of a face — a long, thin piece of bark for a nose, perhaps, or teeth made from the scales of fir cones or flattish seed pods, or fuzzy lichen for eyebrows or a moustache. Arrange the details of the face and glue into place. Allow to dry.

Glue the curly wood shavings into place as hair.

Shingle Owl

INGREDIENTS
piece of firm cardboard, approx.
20 x 25cm (8 x 10in)
flat pieces of different-coloured soft bark,
ranging from dark brown to cream

craft glue
EQUIPMENT
picture of an owl, as reference
pencil
scissors
toothpick

Using the pencil, either trace or draw freehand the outline of an owl onto the cardboard. Mark out two circles for the eyes, a pointed triangular shape for the beak, the wing shapes and a round tummy.

Now cut out different-sized semi-circular shapes from the coloured bark, and sort them into small pale pieces and larger dark pieces, for instance. These 'shingle' shapes will form the owl's feathers.

Arrange the bark pieces in the different sections of the owl. For instance, the small creamy pieces could be placed, overlapping like tiles, on the tummy, while the longer, dark pieces could be placed, overlapping like tiles, up and down the wings. Starting at one side of each eye ring, work around with the medium brown or yellowish pieces of bark, placing each piece over the other. Make the beak from a small pointed chip of wood so that it actually stands out from the rest of the picture.

Once you have finished arranging where the bark pieces will go, pick them up, one by one, add a dab of glue to the square end with the toothpick, and press the pieces in place. Glue down the beak.

Snipped Straw Parrot

INGREDIENTS
**piece of firm cardboard, approx.
25cm (10in) square
different types of straw, thick and thin
watermelon seeds (washed
and dried well)
curved black-eyed beans
wallpaper paste
red, blue and green powder paints**
EQUIPMENT
**picture of a parrot, as reference
pencil
scissors
3 shallow plastic containers**

Using the picture as a guide, trace or freehand draw a parrot onto the piece of cardboard with the pencil.

Snip the straw to different lengths, some only 1.5cm (½in) long, others 2.5cm (1in). With very thick pieces of straw, you may need to cut the straw along its length and open it out, before cutting it into simple strips and geometric shapes.

Move the different types of straw around on the drawing until you are happy with the arrangement. For instance, use the longer pieces of snipped straw as feathers for the parrot's wings and tail, and use the short bits around his face. Use the watermelon seeds to make a beak and eyes, and the curved beans to make the claws.

Divide the wallpaper paste into three portions, in the three containers. Add 2 teaspoons of the different powder paints to each and mix, to make three different-coloured lots of paste.

Working quickly, 'paint' the parrot with the coloured paste, perhaps giving him a red tummy, green head and blue wings. Place the pieces of snipped straw onto the glued surface, one section at a time, following the design you made. Leave to dry thoroughly.

Variation: Press a selection of different types of dried grasses and pieces of straw into a piece of clay or dough about 1.5cm (½in) thick. Make a hole in the top to hang it by, and allow it all to dry.

Bark Giraffe

INGREDIENTS
**piece or thin white cardboard,
30 x 45cm (12 x 18in)
pieces of firm, soft brown bark
craft glue
dried flowers and feathery grasses,
such as barley**
EQUIPMENT
**picture of a giraffe, as reference
pencil
scissors**

Draw a light outline of a giraffe on the cardboard with the pencil. Cut the bark into small pieces.

Glue each piece and stick it inside the outline of the giraffe, like a jigsaw. Fill any gap with tiny leftover snippets of bark. Draw the giraffe's eye and mouth. Make his mane and tail from tufts of the feathery grasses and glue on.

Use the rest of the dried flowers and grasses to make a scene around the giraffe.

Bark Rubbings

INGREDIENTS
several sheets of white paper
thick wax crayon
EQUIPMENT
sticky tape

Take all the materials and go outside in the garden or to a nearby park.

Tape the pieces of paper over the trunks of different trees and bushes. Be careful not to tape paper over jagged bits of trunk that will tear the paper. Gently rub the crayon over the paper, and you will see the bark's pattern appear in relief.

When you have finished with all the different pieces of paper, spread them out and compare them. Trim the edges and, with the help of a reference book, write under each bark rubbing the names of the different types of trees or bushes, for example, pine or gum.

Note for the grown-ups: The next few projects are more appropriate for older children as they use hot glue, a craft knife and clear spray varnish. Supervision and help may be required.

Picture Frame

INGREDIENTS
2 sheets of thick cardboard
selection of different-shaped twigs, dried grasses, tiny pebbles, feathers, dried seed pods and miniature pine cones,
dried flower heads
craft glue
clear spray varnish
EQUIPMENT
pencil
ruler
adjustable craft knife

Draw two identical rectangular shapes, 10 x 15cm (4 x 6in), on the cardboard, using the pencil, then cut them out with the craft knife. On one rectangle draw a smaller central rectangle, 6 x 11cm ($2\frac{1}{2}$ x $4\frac{1}{2}$in). Cut out this shape.

Decorate the frame by gluing on the twigs, dried grasses, pebbles, feathers and seed pods, arranging them in a pattern. Spray with the varnish and allow to dry.

Run a strip of glue around the top and both sides of the solid rectangle, and press the decorated frame down firmly. Slide a photograph or picture through the open slit in the bottom of the frame.

Candle Holders

INGREDIENTS
balsa wood
selection of gumnuts, twigs, acorns, dried berries,
pine cones, pebbles, unshelled nuts,
curly bits of bark
craft glue
clear spray varnish
reusable adhesive, e.g. Blu-Tack,
or modelling clay
2 candles
EQUIPMENT
pencil
compass
sharp knife

Using the pencil and compass, draw two circles, each approximately 2.5cm (5in) in diameter, on the balsa wood. Use the sharp knife to cut out the two circles. In the middle of each piece of wood, pencil a circle where the candle will go, and leave this free.

Decorate the base of each holder with a thick ring-like layer (approx. 2.5cm/1in high all round) of the gumnuts, acorns, berries, twigs and bark, arranging them to form a pattern. (The idea is to make a thick 'wall' of the decorative material, which will go right up to the sides of the candle and so help to keep it in place, and also mask the base where the reusable adhesive will go.) Spray with the clear varnish and allow to dry.

To secure the candles, place a piece of reusable adhesive or modelling clay in the centre of each decorative ring and press the candle base firmly into it.

Wreath

INGREDIENTS

about 20 lengths of creeper or soft stems, such as grape
vines, wisteria, willow or birch, all about
30–45cm (12–18in) long

TO DECORATE:

ribbon, 2.5cm (1in) wide and 90cm (3ft) long and/or
tiny sprigs and clusters of herbs, flowers and grasses
seed pods, such as gumnuts, casuarina, small pine cones,
poppy seed cases
everlasting flowers, such as chamomile daisies,
gypsophila, hydrangea
whole spices, such as nutmegs, star anise, vanilla pods
unshelled nuts, such as almonds
narrow ribbon
clear spray varnish (optional)

Reserve two or three of the longest pieces of creeper and set
them aside. Take about eight pieces of creeper and weave and
twist together to form a long, curved sausage shape. Stretch,
twist and tuck the pieces in and under until the ends nearly
meet to form a circle. Repeat with another eight strands.

Weave and twist the ends of the two curved sausage
shapes together so that the join of one circle is in the centre
of the other. Take the longer, reserved pieces and wind each
firmly around the wreath, tucking the ends under and in.

Take a long piece of the wide ribbon and bind evenly
around the wreath, stitching or gluing the ends.
Alternatively, tuck the tiny bundles of flowers, spices, nuts,
grasses and seeds into the wreath. Start at one side and work
around; this way, the decorations will all travel in the same
direction and overlap to conceal the stems.

Make a loop from the narrow ribbon and stitch it to the
top of the wreath to hang it up by. Set the wreath aside to dry
thoroughly. If you have not used ribbon, you might like to
spray the wreath with clear varnish when it is quite dry.

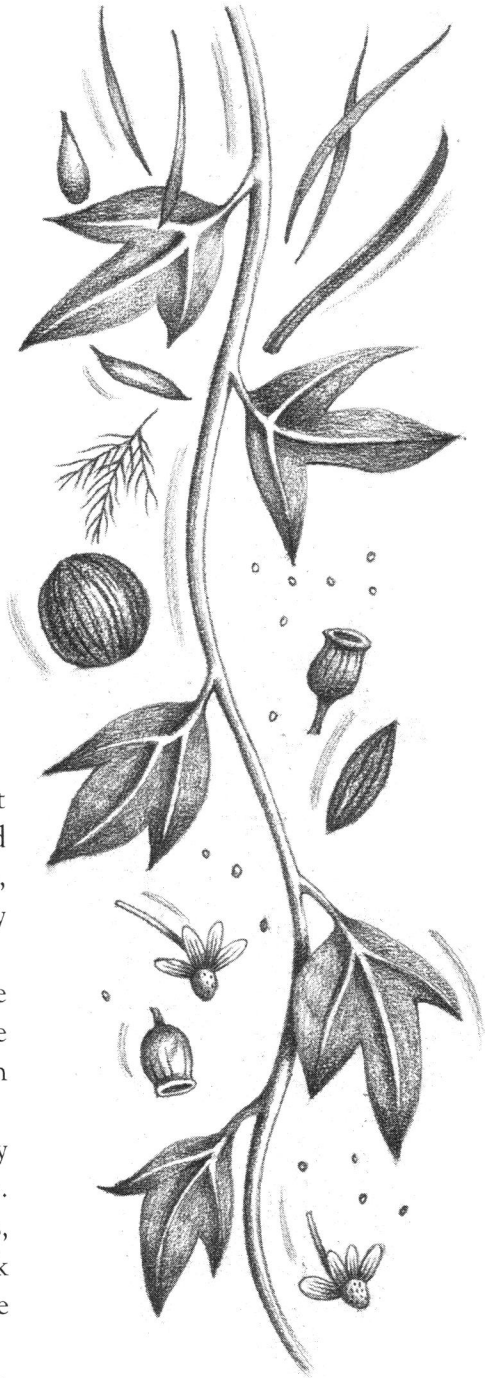

Making a Wreath

Woven Wallhanging

INGREDIENTS
**corrugated cardboard, 45cm
(18in) square
string, yarn or raffia
collection of nuts, feathers, dried twigs
and flowers, shells, dried ferns, thistles,
grasses, seed heads
fuse wire
craft glue**
EQUIPMENT
**pencil
ruler
scissors
stapler**

With the pencil and ruler, measure and mark 2.5cm (1in) intervals along all four sides of the cardboard square. Use the scissors to cut 1.5cm ($\frac{1}{2}$in) notches at these points.

Take lengths of string, yarn or raffia and tie them around the cardboard at notches opposite each other. Repeat, this time going across the warp (the other way), weaving in and out to create a mesh-like effect.

Now you have a firm, woven backing to decorate. Wire together clusters of nuts and seeds and tie them on. Tie or glue on the feathers, shells or twigs, and weave the lengths of grass and long pieces of fern over and under the pieces of string.

Tie or staple an extra length of string or raffia to the top of the cardboard to hang up the finished work.

Twig Jumper

INGREDIENTS
**small, thin, Y-shaped forked twig,
approx. 12.5cm (5in) long
thick strong rubber band
small straight twig, approx. 5cm (2in)
long**

Stretch the rubber band across the tops of the forked twig, then loop the small straight twig between the two sides midway. The straight twig should be short enough to just miss the join of the fork.

Wind the straight twig up, 10–15 twists should do it, and then hold the straight twig down on a flat surface. Quickly raise your hand so that the straight twig spins around, making the whole thing jump in the air, land, and jump up again.

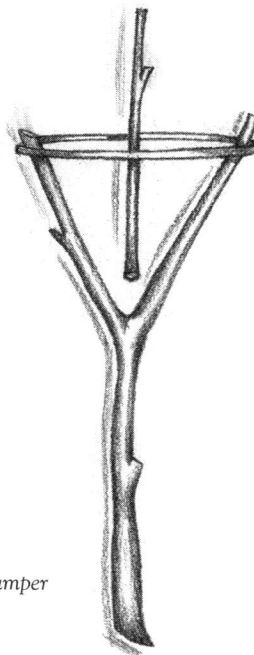

Twig Jumper

SEEDS AND NUTS

There is something truly magical about even the smallest seed or nut — so tiny, yet such a little powerhouse, with a whole plant or even a tree locked away inside it! They are also wonderful materials to use in crafty pursuits. Use them to make Christmas decorations, or lovely jewellery.

Remember, though, that some nuts and seeds can be poisonous, so make sure than none are left where smaller children could put them in their mouths. Also, the first couple of projects involve the use of a hot-glue gun, so an adult will have to supervise.

Nut Pyramid

These nut pyramids make great table centrepieces for a Christmas table. Or they can be used as place markers — write the names of your family on cards and prop one against each nut pyramid next to their place.

INGREDIENTS

medium-weight cardboard, approx. 18 x 40cm (7 x 16in)
selection of nuts in their shells, e.g. walnuts, almonds, peanuts, hazelnuts
craft glue

EQUIPMENT

stapler
newspaper
hot-glue gun

Roll the cardboard to form a cone approximately 18cm (7in) high, and glue and staple the seam to secure. Place the cone on a piece of newspaper.

Glue a ring of larger nuts, such as walnuts, around the base of the cone. Then glue a row of almonds, moving up the cone with contrasting rows of almonds, peanuts, hazelnuts

I had a little nut tree

Nothing would it bear

But a silver nutmeg and

a golden pear

The King of Spain's daughter

Came to visit me

And all for the sake of

my little nut tree.

and so on. Fill in all the gaps so that no cardboard shows. Use the hot-glue gun to secure the heavier nuts, like walnuts.

Gilded Walnuts

This traditional Christmas tree ornament dates back to 17th-century England.

INGREDIENTS
walnut shell halves
metallic gold-coloured enamel paint
gold thread
beads
EQUIPMENT
rubber gloves
large plastic or foil container
newspaper
old cake racks
darning needle

Put on the gloves to protect your hands and pour the paint into the large container. Spread out several layers of newspaper for drying the shells on. Dip the shells into the enamel, one at a time, then place them face down on the old cake racks on the newspaper to drip dry.

When they are quite dry, thread the darning needle with the gold thread and pierce the shells near the top to string them. To stop the shells clustering together, thread beads in between them, or tie knots in the thread on either side of the shells to space them out more evenly.

Nut Ball or Tree

INGREDIENTS
foam ball, 7.5cm (3in) diameter
nuts, e.g. chestnuts, walnuts, almonds, Brazil nuts, unshelled peanuts, pecans
spices, e.g. whole nutmegs, whole cloves, allspice berries, dried miniature pine cones, cinnamon sticks
ribbon
thin dowelling, 23cm (9in) long
modelling clay
small terracotta pot
pebbles or sand
EQUIPMENT
hot-glue gun

Working carefully round the ball, fix on rows of nuts by dabbing a drop of hot glue on each. Try to create a decorative pattern. Then work around the ball again, carefully gluing and inserting different spices between the nuts to cover the entire surface of foam. To hang the nut ball, glue a loop of ribbon to the top.

If you want to make a nut tree instead, first stick the piece of dowelling into the foam ball, inserting it about 5cm (2in) so that it is firm. Then secure the other end of the dowelling into the modelling clay in the base of the pot, and fill in with pebbles or sand. Decorate the ball with the nuts.

Walnut Cradles

*Walnut cradles make beautiful
Christmas tree decorations.*

INGREDIENTS
**clean walnut shell halves
cottonwool
tiny baby dolls
scraps of cotton, felt or wool
craft glue
gold string**
EQUIPMENT
scissors

Clean out each walnut half and tuck in
a small 'mattress' of cottonwool. Place a
small baby doll on top of the mattress. Cut
a blanket and sheet from the scraps of
cotton, felt or wool. Glue the sides of
the 'bedclothes' and use them to tuck the
baby in.

Walnut cradles may be hung up by
gluing a small loop of gold string to the
top end.

Walnut Cradle

Walnut Ships

*Making walnut ships is a good project for
Christmas time, when there are bound to be
plenty of walnut shells around. Make two or
three and race them in the bath!*

INGREDIENTS
**walnut shell halves
reusable adhesive, e.g. Blu-Tack
paper
felt-tip pens
toothpick
craft glue**
EQUIPMENT
scissors

Press a large piece of reusable adhesive into
the base of each shell. Then make a sail by
cutting out a triangle of paper, approximately
2.5cm (1in) long. Decorate the sail, if you
like, with a skull-and-crossbones, or a cross
or sun. Then glue the sail to a toothpick
and stick the bottom of the toothpick into
the reusable adhesive.

Now cut out a small anchor from paper
and glue that to the side of the ship.

Walnut Ship

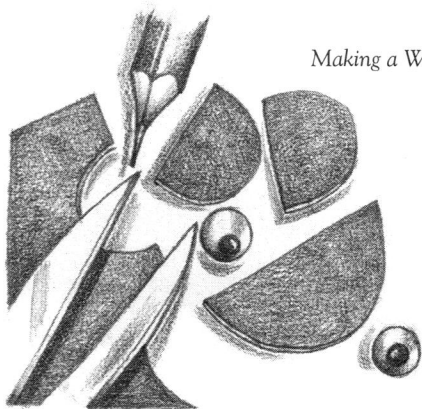

Walnut Turtle

INGREDIENTS
walnut shell half
brown, black and green poster paints
fine black felt-tip pen
fine cardboard
craft glue
purchased wobbly eyes (from craft shop
or hobby shop)
EQUIPMENT
scissors
paintbrush

Paint the shell to resemble a turtle's shell — black or brown with a pattern of green squarish shapes. Set the shell aside to dry.

Cut out four small semi-circles and one larger one from the cardboard. These will be the turtle's feet and head. Paint the feet brown and pick out toes and claws with black. Glue the feet to the underside of the turtle's shell.

Paint the head brown and stick on wobbly eyes, then glue the neck edge to the underside of the shell.

Making a Walnut Turtle

I love to go for a walk in a park and collect gumnuts that have fallen. They come in many different shapes and sizes — some long or oval, others dear little round balls. They all smell beautifully, too, of eucalyptus! Never collect gumnuts in a national park, as removing anything (apart from your rubbish!) from a national park is not allowed.

If you don't have gum trees growing near you, you might be able to find other nuts, such as acorns, hazelnuts or pecans, that would be suitable for some of these projects. Or you could buy gumnuts from a craft shop. Make sure, though, if you are planning on making the bubble pipe, that the gumnuts haven't been impregnated with eucalyptus oil.

Eucalyptus Jar

INGREDIENTS
different-shaped gumnuts and gum leaves
clean glass jar
eucalyptus or lemon eucalyptus essential
oil (from health food or
department stores)
muslin or sprigged cotton
rubber band
ribbon
EQUIPMENT
pinking shears

Crush the leaves slightly. Place the nuts and leaves in a clean glass jar and sprinkle with a little essential oil.

Make a pretty 'cap' for the jar by cutting out a circle of muslin or sprigged cotton with the pinking shears and placing it over the top of the jar. Secure it with a rubber band, then tie a ribbon around and finish with a bow so that the muslin or cotton stands out like a frill.

Keep the jar in your bedroom or bathroom, where it will fill the air with the sharp scent of eucalyptus.

Note for the grown-ups: You will have to be on hand for this activity, as it involves the use of a penknife.

Gumnut Bubble Pipe

We sat out on the back verandah, the boys and I, and blew beautiful soap bubbles. Randall whooped and hollered with delight, jumping and pointing and squealing. Edward, older, solemnly practised his bubble blowing over and over till he made a simply enormous one, which floated up and up and up, almost over the top of the crepe myrtle tree. Where has all the time gone? It's true what people say when you have babies — they only stay little for such a short time. Bubble blowing on the back verandah is one of the small treasures I remember.

INGREDIENTS
large gumnut
hollow bamboo, about 6mm (¼in)
diameter and 15cm (6in) long
water-resistant sealant
gloss paint or clear varnish (optional)
EQUIPMENT
penknife
awl
knitting needle or skewer

Clean out the inside of the gumnut with the penknife to make the base of the pipe. Make a hole in the side of the gumnut using the point of the penknife or an awl. (The spot where the nut was attached to its stem is usually the softest.) Push in the bamboo stem, sealing with a thin strip of the water-resistant sealant. Allow to dry.

Scrape out the inside of the bamboo with the knitting needle or skewer till it is quite smooth. Decorate the bubble pipe with bright gloss paint or clear varnish if you wish.

To blow bubbles, dip the pipe into a dish of soapy water and blow gently.

Seed pods

Seed Pod Showers

INGREDIENTS
2 old wire coathangers
fuse wire
silver spray paint
clusters of hard seed pods, e.g. gumnuts,
casuarina pods, poppy seed heads, acorns
or banksia pods, or hard berries on twigs
clear spray varnish
glitter
silver thread
EQUIPMENT
newspaper

First, make a frame from which to hang the seed pod showers by wiring the coathangers together at their hooks, then turning the bases at right angles to each other. Place the frame on newspaper and spray with silver paint. Allow to dry.

Divide the clusters of seed pods and spread them out on two sections of newspaper. Spray one half with the silver paint, and allow to dry. Spray the other half with the clear varnish and sprinkle liberally with the glitter; repeat, if necessary.

When both sets of seed pods are dry, tie bunches to different lengths of silver thread and tie to the frame. The idea is to hang them at different lengths, to create a scattered 'showery' effect, rather than have them at all the same lengths.

Hang the seed pod shower from a lampshade, or in a window where it will move in a breeze.

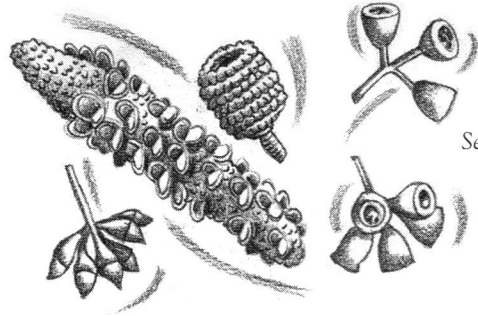

Nutty Fridge Magnet

INGREDIENTS
tiny gumnuts, hazelnuts or pecans
gum leaves or bay leaves
clear spray varnish
thick pink or pale green cardboard
craft glue
dark green or pink paint
purchased flat magnet
EQUIPMENT
scrap paper or newspaper
scissors
fine paintbrush

Spread gumnuts and leaves out on a piece of scrap paper or newspaper and spray with clear varnish; allow to dry.

Cut out a small heart or circular shape from the thick cardboard. When the gumnuts and leaves are dry, glue them to the cardboard shape in a pattern. Decorate the edges of the shapes with fine lines or dots of green or pink paint.

When the magnet decoration is quite dry, turn it over and glue the flat magnet to the centre of the back. Allow to dry thoroughly.

Note for the grown-ups: Making plaster can be a pretty messy business although it is quite straightforward. Unless children have made up plaster before, adult supervision is definitely required. As with most of the projects in this book, it is also a good idea to spread out plenty of newspaper beforehand.

Nut Shadow Paperweight

INGREDIENTS
casting plaster (from hardware stores)
selection of unshelled nuts with different shapes,
e.g. almonds, walnuts, peanuts, hazelnuts, gumnuts
purchased flat magnet or fine ribbon
craft glue
EQUIPMENT
ice-cream container
old spoon or straight stick
small foil patty pans
paperclip

Make up the casting plaster in the old ice-cream container according to the manufacturer's instructions, using the old spoon or the stick to mix. (Remember: You will not be able to use the spoon again.)

Pour the plaster into the foil patty pans, to within about 6mm ($\frac{1}{4}$in) of the rim. It will start to firm up almost immediately, so work quickly. To make interesting-shaped 'shadows', press different nuts into the plaster for a few moments, then take them away.

Leave the plaster to dry overnight. Peel off the patty pan cases. Either glue the flat magnet to the back and use as a fridge magnet, or place the opened-out paperclip in the plaster mix before setting it aside to dry. When you remove this, you will have a hole through which to thread a fine ribbon. Use it to hang up the 'paperweight'.

Peanut Puppets

I remember making peanut puppets in my Nanna's house when I was about nine. We set up the clothes horse as a stage by draping pillowslips and old sheets over it as 'curtains', and then made our puppets dance and play to the accompaniment of our silly jokes and songs. A really absorbing project for a rainy day indoors.

INGREDIENTS
3 ice-block sticks
craft glue
unshelled peanuts
strong thread
wool
poster paints or felt-tip pens
EQUIPMENT
needle
paintbrush

Glue together two ice-block sticks crosswise. Set aside and let the glue dry — this will be the control handle.

Select four small peanuts (for hands and feet), eight medium ones (to make arms and legs) and three large ones (two for the body, one for the neck and head).

Thread the peanuts together as follows: first tie a big knot in a long piece of the strong thread, then thread through a small peanut for the foot, up through two medium ones for a leg, and up through the three large ones for the head and body. Leave a long thread above the head.

Repeat with another foot and leg, then pass this second thread up through to the head too. Repeat with the arms, thread through the top of the body and up through the head.

Tie off all but one of the threads through the top of the head. Attach a control thread to the two hands and two feet and tie these to each of the four ends of the crosswise sticks. Tie the central one from the head to the centre stick. Put a

Making Peanut Puppets

THE WISHING TREE

couple of dabs of glue on the control stick where the threads are tied to stop them from slipping.

Glue the wool to the peanut puppet's head for hair, and give him a face with the paints or felt-tip pens.

Nut or seed jewellery pieces make great presents for people at Christmas. Another good idea is to get together with other children and make gumnut or acorn brooches and sell them to friends and family as a way of raising money for your school. Younger children will need supervision and help for this project.

Seed Necklaces

INGREDIENTS
**seeds, such as melon or sunflower, or beech
strong thread
gloss paints in different colours**
EQUIPMENT
**fine-mesh drying rack
scissors
thick sewing needle
newspaper
paintbrush**

Wash and dry the seeds thoroughly, spreading them out on the drying rack in the sun for at least a day.

Cut a piece of strong thread about

Colouring Seeds

Another simpler idea for colouring the seeds is to soak them overnight in a shallow pot or small cup with a mixture of water and food colouring. The seeds then need to be left on a rack to dry thoroughly.

60cm (2ft) long. Thread the needle, tie a knot at one end and then very carefully push it through the middle or top half of the first seed. Continue until you have threaded all the seeds onto the thread, then tie the two ends together.

Lay the necklace on several sheets of newspaper and paint one side of all the seeds with the gloss paints — using the different colours to create a stripy effect will look good. Hang the necklace up to dry.

When it is dry, place it painted side down on newspaper and repeat the process, mixing and matching the paint colours to give a really colourful finish. Hang the necklace up to dry again.

Variation: Make a necklace by threading popcorn and large seeds, such as melon and sunflower seeds, onto thread. Or thread triangles of cardboard together and glue on seeds to make a pattern. If you want to make a bracelet, thread the seeds on shirring elastic instead of thread.

Gumnut or Acorn Brooch

INGREDIENTS
cluster of small gumnuts or acorns
several gum leaves or bay leaves
florist's wire or fuse wire
craft glue
clear spray varnish
safety clasp or brooch pin
(from craft stores)

Arrange the gumnuts or acorns and leaves together in an attractive spray. Bind the stems of the leaves together tightly with fuse wire, and wire or glue the gumnuts in place. Spray the arrangement with the varnish and allow to dry.

Thread an additional length of wire through the bound section and through the holes in the clasp or brooch pin, twisting the ends tightly together. Make sure you cannot see the clasp from the front.

Ear-wings

Seeds have lots of different ways of getting around. Some of them have hooks or prickles to hitch a ride on people or animals. Some of them have wings, which help them to glide or spin in the air or float on water.

INGREDIENTS
winged seeds, such as sycamore
or ash seeds
small round nuts or seed heads, such as
acorns, rosehips, gumnuts
purchased earring clips
craft glue
clear varnish
EQUIPMENT
paintbrush

Select two nut or seed heads that are very similar in size and colour for the base of the earrings. Then choose two paired winged sycamore or ash seeds that are the same size and colour.

Open out the claw attachment at the base of one of the earring clips, glue and fit over the top of the nut or seed head. Allow to dry. Glue sycamore or ash seed 'wings' to the top half of the front of the nut or seed head. Allow to dry.

Paint the entire decoration with a thick coat of clear varnish. This will help to preserve the nut and stop the wings from being broken or cracked.

Repeat with the other earring clip.

Keep an eye out for seeds and seed pods wherever you go, and get into the habit of collecting them. In the garden, shake the heads of plants that have gone to seed, or save the seeds from tomatoes, grapes, pumpkins or watermelons that have been bought from the greengrocer. It will be easy to grow these plants from seed and it can save quite a lot of money!

Secret Seed Box

Seeds come in so many interesting shapes and colours and sizes. If you have a collection, use them to cover a special box which you can use to store ... more seeds!

INGREDIENTS
small cardboard box with lid
craft glue
seeds, e.g. orange pips, sunflower seeds, apple pips,
melon seeds, lentils, mung beans, split peas
clear varnish
EQUIPMENT
paintbrush

Sort out the seeds according to size and colour. Paint the outside of the box with glue, then press the seeds into the glue in a decorative pattern — stripes look terrific. Then do the same to the lid.

Leave the box and lid to dry overnight, then paint them with a clear varnish to protect the seeds and bring out their natural colours.

Seedy Stones

Large seedy stones can be used as paperweights, which make good gifts for grandparents.

INGREDIENTS
**smooth round stones or pebbles
craft glue
collection of different-coloured seeds,
dried beans or rice
clear varnish**
EQUIPMENT
**chalk
paintbrush**

Sharpen the end of the chalk and sketch a design on each of the stones — different-sized circles or wavy lines will both look good. Spread the glue along the lines of the design and then decorate the stone by pressing the seeds or beans onto the glue.

When the stone is dry, paint it with clear varnish.

Birdseed Squiggle Pictures

INGREDIENTS
**piece of thin cardboard, approx. 45cm
(18in) square
selection of different grades of birdseed
(different shapes and sizes will give the
picture contrast)
craft glue
powder paints**

EQUIPMENT
**pencil
plastic bag
rubber band
paintbrush**

Sketch out a pattern of squiggly lines on the cardboard. Plan which lines are going to be coloured, and where the bigger and smaller seeds will go.

Half-fill the plastic bag with the seeds and 2–3 tablespoons of powder paint. Seal the bag with the rubber band and shake it vigorously to mix the colour thoroughly with the seed.

Taking one squiggly line at a time, apply the glue. Then sprinkle the coloured seeds onto that section and shake them off.

Allow the glue to dry, then repeat the process with the other squiggles.

Bean Shaker

INGREDIENTS
**dried beans
dried macaroni
jar or container with lid, e.g. plastic
bottle, coffee jar
coloured adhesive paper or piece of old
wrapping paper
craft glue
felt-tip pens (optional)
clear spray varnish**

Put the beans and macaroni in the jar or container and put the lid on. Cover the container with the coloured adhesive paper, or glue the wrapping paper around it; make sure the lid is covered, too. Use the felt-tip pens to decorate the shaker with your initials or a picture if you like. Set aside to dry.

When the shaker is dry, spray it with two or three coats of the clear varnish.

Amazing Bean Bottle

INGREDIENTS
spaghetti jar or other long, narrow glass jar
selection of beans, e.g. pinto beans, peppercorns, fennel seeds, popcorn (unpopped), coriander seeds, split peas, black-eyed beans, coffee beans, lima beans, kidney beans

Wash and dry the spaghetti jar. Pour in layers of the beans, each about 4cm (1½in) high, one after the other. Arrange the layers so that you have interesting contrasts of shapes, texture and colours.

Bean Bags

Tossing bean bags in games like 'hot potato' is a very old custom. There are frescoes in ancient Greek temples that show boys filling little bags with what look like lentils, and then throwing them around a circle of players. They are very easy to make.

INGREDIENTS
rag-bag scraps of felt or fine corduroy
strong thread
lentils or dried black-eyed beans
felt-tip pens (optional)
EQUIPMENT
scissors
needle

Cut two pieces from the felt or corduroy, each about 7.5cm (3in) square. Place the pieces face to face, stitch up three sides, turn right side out and fill with a tablespoon or so of the lentils or black-eyed beans. Stitch up the fourth seam.

You can decorate your bean bag with your initials or an appliqué shape of an animal, if you would like to make it especially yours.

STONES

That first rock collection can turn into a lifelong interest. (My husband still has fun identifying the different types of rocks our sons find when we go for walks, and says he has his geography teacher to thank for getting him interested in this area!) It is simple and easy to build a rock collection, and children can learn to identify different rocks and pebbles by looking them up in a book on geology from the library. They are also very pretty to look at and work with — projects like making the Pebble People here can be great fun for a junior 'rock enthusiast'!

Rock Collection

INGREDIENTS
12 matchboxes
craft glue
red or blue poster paint
selection of small rocks and pebbles
roll of cottonwool
thin cardboard
fine felt-tip pen
EQUIPMENT
paintbrush
scissors

Remove the covers of the matchboxes and glue the sides of the inners together to make 12 separate compartments. Paint the inside and outside of the boxes and leave overnight to dry thoroughly.

Cut a flat piece of cottonwool to line each box. Wash and dry the rocks and pebbles, sort according to size, colour, shape and/or type (e.g. quartz, slate, shale) and place in the different boxes.

Cut out small cardboard rectangles and, using the felt-tip pen, write on each rectangle the name of a different kind of

And we will all the

pleasures prove

That valleys, groves, hills

and fields,

Woods or steepy mountain yields.

CHRISTOPHER MARLOWE, 'THE PASSIONATE

SHEPHERD TO HIS LOVE' (1589)

rock in the collection. Prop the rectangles up in the appropriate sections.

Variation: An egg carton is another really good way to display a collection of tiny rocks or pebbles. Line each cup with cottonwool, and tape notes in front telling where you found each piece.

Note for the grown-ups: It's a good idea to spread out newspaper before beginning any activities involving paint and spray varnish.

Painted Stones

INGREDIENTS
selection of stones
poster paints or tempera paints
clear varnish
EQUIPMENT
flat bristle brushes

Wash the stones thoroughly in water, as paint will not adhere to a greasy surface. Allow them to dry thoroughly.

If you like, you can just scoop up paint with your fingers and spread it over the stones. Or you can paint on designs of your choice with a brush; an animal's face or a monster may be suggested by a certain shape.

Experiment with painted effects — paint does not always have to be brushed on. It may be sprayed on by holding a brushful of paint next to a stone and blowing at it, it can be dripped straight onto a stone, or tiny little dots can be

stippled all over a stone's surface with an almost-dry brush.

When the stones are quite dry, paint them with the clear varnish.

If you have collected a pile of stones and pebbles, you might want to make something with them. Spend some time figuring out what you want to make and how you want to put it together.

Pebble Fruit

INGREDIENTS
selection of different-shaped pebbles
poster paints or tempera paints
clear varnish
thin cardboard
craft glue
green pipe-cleaners
EQUIPMENT
paintbrush

Have a good look at the different pebbles. Is there a round one with a little dent on top? That can be an apple. Paint it red, then give it a coat of clear varnish. When it is dry, glue on a leaf made from cardboard, coloured green.

What about grapes? Are there a lot of small, perfectly round pebbles? Paint them green or purple, glue them together in a bunch and make twirling vines out of a green pipe-cleaner. Give the bunch of

grapes some leaves cut out of cardboard too.

Now, what about making an orange, or a little triangular strawberry or an oval lemon or a knobbly-looking blackberry …? A really big heavy-looking pebble or stone could be a melon.

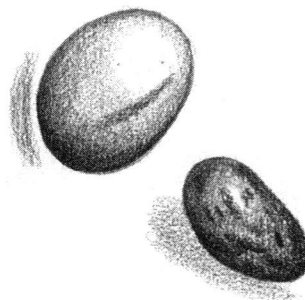

Pebble People

INGREDIENTS
**selection of pebbles — large and oval for the bodies, small and flat for the feet and round for the head
craft glue
poster paints or tempera paints
clear varnish
wool or string
scraps of coloured felt**
EQUIPMENT
**fine paintbrush
scissors**

Wash and dry the pebbles thoroughly before use, as paint will not adhere to a greasy surface.

Select a large oval pebble for a body and put some glue on the places where you will fix the feet. Put glue on the tops of two small flat pebbles, then press these 'feet' into position. Leave to stand and dry, supported by other objects if necessary. When dry, glue on the head pebble in the same way.

Decorate your pebble person by painting on a face, clothes and arms.

When the paint is dry, paint the pebble person with the clear varnish. Set aside to dry. Now glue lengths of wool or string to the head as hair, or make a cap or hat from felt.

Pebble Puppy

INGREDIENTS
**selection of small, spotted pebbles — a large sausage-shaped one for the body, a round one for the head and small flat ones for the legs, ears and tail
craft glue
black felt-tip pen
clear spray varnish
moveable eyes (from craft stores)
narrow strip of black felt, or black pipe-cleaner**

Glue the pebbles together to form the puppy. Darken any of the spots on the pebbles with the felt-tip pen if they need it, or if you haven't been able to find spotted pebbles, make your own spots! Spray the puppy with clear varnish and allow to dry.

Glue on the eyes and a strip of black felt or a black pipe-cleaner to make the Pebble Puppy's tail.

THE WISHING TREE

Stone Paperweight Monster

INGREDIENTS
**selection of stones and pebbles of
different sizes and shapes
tempera paints
craft glue
clear varnish
scraps of coloured felt**
EQUIPMENT
**paintbrush
scissors**

Wash and dry all the stones and pebbles to remove any dirt or grease.

Arrange them to form a crazy monster — one or two large stones to make the body, a roundish pebble for the head and smaller flat pebbles for the feet. Once you have a shape you are happy with, glue all the pieces together.

Use the tempera paints to mark eyes, nose and a great big mouth full of teeth. When dry, paint the monster with clear varnish.

Cut out ears and a mane from the felt and glue them onto the monster's head, then cut out a tail and glue that on too.

Pebbles come in many forms and shapes, and many have beautiful markings and colourings, which can be used to great effect in the following projects.

Pebble Medallions

INGREDIENTS
**heavy cardboard
poster paints or felt-tip pens
8–10 small, different-shaped pebbles
clear varnish
craft glue
leather thonging or ribbon**
EQUIPMENT
**scissors
paintbrush
skewer**

Cut out 8–10 round medallions from the cardboard, each approximately 2.5cm (1in) in diameter. Use the poster paints or the felt-tip pens to colour both sides.

Mark two points, at '11 o'clock' and '1 o'clock' on each medallion, and use the skewer to punch holes at these points.

Paint the pebbles with the clear varnish and allow to dry. Glue the pebbles onto the medallions and allow to dry. Thread leather thonging or ribbon through the medallion holes so that they will lie flat. Tie the ribbon so that the medallions can be worn.

River Secrets Box

A walk along a creek bed or by a river can yield the most extraordinary collection of tiny, rounded pebbles and pretty 'river rocks'. I always think they must be very wise, having listened to the chatter of the water for so many years.

INGREDIENTS
matchbox
piece of felt
silicon glue
small packet of plaster
selection of little rounded pebbles and tiny chips of river gravel — look for different colours and shapes to give contrast
clear spray varnish
EQUIPMENT
pencil
scissors
plastic ice-cream container
old butter knife or spatula

Take out the inner sleeve of the matchbox. Place the matchbox outer on the piece of felt and trace neatly around it. Cut out a rectangle of felt and, using a thin line of silicon glue right around the edge, stick the felt to the base of the outer.

Mix up the plaster in the ice-cream container according to the manufacturer's instructions. Using the old butter knife or spatula, coat the top and sides of the outer with the plaster. Gently press the little rocks and pebbles into the plaster in a design, as thickly and closely as possible; don't leave any sections of plaster uncovered. Set the outer aside and allow to dry.

Spray the outer thoroughly with clear varnish and allow to dry. Reinsert the inner drawer, and use this box to keep something very special and small in.

Stone Mosaic

INGREDIENTS

selection of small stones and pebbles
300g (9½oz) fine-grained sand
1 cup (250ml/8fl oz) white glue
extra 2–3 tablespoons of sand

EQUIPMENT
plastic pie dish or straight-edged
container, approx. 30cm (12in) diameter
aluminium foil

Line the pie dish or straight-edged container with the foil, pressing it up and around the sides. Wash and dry the stones and pebbles carefully.

Make a cement by mixing the sand and glue together to form a thick paste, adding a little extra glue if necessary.

Cover the bottom of the pie dish with the cement to a depth of about 2cm (¾in). Press the stones into the cement in a pattern. Sprinkle lightly with the extra sand and let the mosaic set overnight.

The next day, carefully tip the mosaic out of the container and peel off the foil.

Pebble Game

INGREDIENTS
felt-tip pens
shallow box or lid, about
12.5cm (5in) square
2 sets of three similar-coloured pebbles

Use the felt-tip pens to mark out a nine-square chequerboard pattern on the inside of the lid, three boxes across the top, bottom and sides.

Each player has one set of three pebbles and takes turns to put them down, one at a time, each trying to make a matching row. When all six pebbles are on the chequerboard, the players then take turns to each move a pebble, one at a time, until one 'checks' the other and makes a row of three.

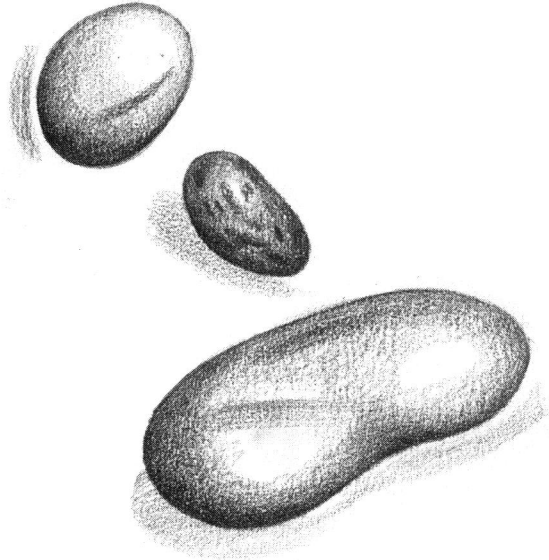

SHELLS

One of my earliest memories is of picking up a shell and being shown how to hold it to my ear so that I could hear the sound of the 'sea'. It was actually a very large old shell that my mother had been given by a relative from Fiji, and we still have it. Lovely big shells like this don't seem to wash up on our beaches as often as they used to, but craft and hobby shops will usually have some pretty ones to sell if you don't often get to the seaside. Anyway, beachcombing will still yield plenty of small, pretty shells which can be used to make projects like the Shell Mosaic and Shell Mirror here.

Shell Mosaic

INGREDIENTS
**sheet of heavy cardboard, about 25cm (10in) square
craft glue
selection of very small, pretty different-coloured shells —
broken pieces are fine
clear varnish**
EQUIPMENT
**pencil
paintbrush**

Draw a design on the cardboard. A simple spiral can look terrific, so can a sun shape.

Spread glue all over the cardboard. Place the biggest pieces of shell on the lines of the design first, then fill in the spaces with the smaller ones. See if you can keep the design one colour, and all the surrounding spaces another.

When you have completed your mosaic, set it aside to dry. If you wish, you can paint some of the shells to highlight them, or just brush the whole work with clear varnish.

Shell Brooch

**large shell with a flattish back
(cowry shells are ideal)
craft glue
clear spray varnish
flat safety clasp or brooch pin
(from craft stores)**

Wash and dry the shell thoroughly. Spray with clear varnish and allow to dry. Glue the clasp or pin to the back of the shell.

Shell Necklace

INGREDIENTS

**flat or spiral cone-shaped shells
bell caps (from craft shop)
craft glue
ribbon, raffia or gold thread**

Arrange the shells in a row, the way that you would like to see them hang on the necklace — the big ones in the middle with the smaller ones off to the sides, for instance. Glue the bell caps to the tops of the shells and allow to dry thoroughly.

Thread the shells onto the raffia, ribbon or gold thread. To stop the shells clumping together, either tie a knot around the bell cap loop of each one as you thread it into position, or tie a knot on each side of the loop to stop it moving.

Mermaid Headband

INGREDIENTS

**strip of green or blue satin, 7.5 x 30cm
(3 x 12in)
fabric stiffening (iron-on is perfect)
sewing thread
piece of elastic, 6mm ($^1/_4$ in) wide
small, pretty shells
craft glue**

EQUIPMENT

needle

Reinforce the satin with the fabric stiffening, according to the manufacturer's instructions. Trim. Fold the satin in half lengthwise with right sides together. Stitch down two sides and turn inside out. Turn in the rough edges and hand sew closed.

Hold the band around the head and measure how much elastic is required at the back so that the band sits snugly across the forehead. Sew the elastic to each end of the satin strip.

Arrange the shells in a decorative pattern and glue them in place.

Shell Mirror

*Perfect for all those little mermaids
out there …*

INGREDIENTS
**small framed hand mirror
selection of small, pretty sea shells
craft glue
soft pink or green paint (optional)
clear varnish**
EQUIPMENT
paintbrush

Glue shells all over the back of the mirror. Set aside to dry. Glue shells around the border of the mirror on the other side, and allow to dry.

If you wish, you could tint the shells with a pale green or pale pink paint; otherwise, just paint them with clear varnish to bring out their natural colours.

Shell Treasure Box

INGREDIENTS
**small lidded wooden box, preferably with
a lock and key (from craft shops)
selection of small, pretty shells
craft glue
clear varnish**
EQUIPMENT
paintbrush

Glue the shells all over the box and lid in a decorative pattern, leaving the area where the lid slides down and the keyhole free from shells.

Set the treasure box aside until the glue is dry, then paint it with clear varnish to bring out the natural colours of the shells.

Shell Plant Pot

INGREDIENTS
**clay or terracotta plant pot
selection of medium and large shells
strong glue, e.g. Araldite
clear varnish**
EQUIPMENT
paintbrush

Glue the shells all around the plant pot in a decorative pattern — you can make a weird face with different-shaped shells for eyebrows and a nose, or the shells' different colours might suggest a pattern to you. Set the pot aside and allow the glue to dry.

To give your finished shell plant pot a shiny look, coat it with clear varnish.

Shell Gardens

INGREDIENTS
**selection of largish shells, with
wide openings
clear spray varnish**

old tray
silicon glue and modelling clay
potting mix
seeds, e.g. viola, alfalfa, mustard-and-cress, watercress

Wash and dry the shells carefully and leave to drain. When dry, spray the outsides with clear varnish to make them shine. Allow to dry.

Set the shells upright on the tray, securing them in place with the silicon glue and modelling clay. (You may have to prop them against an arrangement of some other shells glued together to make them stand upright.)

Fill the shells with potting mix and plant the seeds. Mist lightly with water every day or so, and watch your tiny gardens grow.

Shell Animals

INGREDIENTS
selection of shells of different sizes and shapes,
e.g. small flat ones for ears or feet, round or cone-shaped
ones for bodies or heads
craft glue
acrylic paints
tiny white buttons (optional)
clear varnish
EQUIPMENT
small paintbrush

Start with one big flattish shell or four smaller ones, for either the base or the feet of the animal.

Look at each shell to see if it suggests an animal shape to you — a flat round shell might become a cat or a frog, a squat teardrop-shaped one might be a penguin, while a lumpy big one could be a bear or a walrus.

Glue the shells together to form the animal.

TRY THIS TONGUE TWISTER:

She sells sea shells

by the sea shore ...

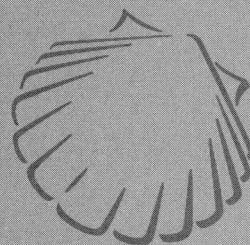

Decorate each animal by painting on its eyes, nose or mouth. Or you can use buttons for eyes. Paint a centre on them and glue them on. When the animal is dry, coat it with clear varnish.

Shell Plaque

INGREDIENTS
small packet of plaster
old dinner or dessert plate
selection of different-sized coloured shells
(flattish ones are best)
tempera paints (optional)
clear spray varnish
purchased picture claw-frame and hook set

EQUIPMENT
plastic ice-cream container
old butter knife or spatula
paintbrush

Mix up the plaster in the ice-cream container according to the manufacturer's instructions.

Pour the plaster into the dinner or dessert plate, smoothing its surface with the knife or spatula. Press the shells gently into the surface of the plaster in a pattern — perhaps a large shell in the centre, surrounded by a spiral of small ones. Set the plate aside for at least a week to allow the plaster to dry thoroughly.

If you wish, decorate the shells with paint. When dry, spray with the clear varnish.

To hang, stretch and hook the claws of the purchased frame over the edges of the plate.

FEATHERS

Even though we live in the city, we are fortunate to have plenty of birds that seem to like our backyard. Perhaps the fact that we have put out a birdbath and that we regularly hang up seed balls has something to do with it! We always seem to be able to find the odd feather in the garden, too. But even if you live in a flat, you should be able to find feathers in a park or a friend's garden. Another good idea is to ask a zoo or bird sanctuary if they will let you have some.

Yankee Doodle came to town

Riding on a pony;

Stuck a feather in his cap

And called it Macaroni.

Quill Pen

For centuries people used turkey or goose quills as pens and, even in the age of ballpoint pens, it is still a fun and romantic thing to do.

Note for the grown-ups: Adult supervision will be required when it comes to cutting the notch in this pen. Use a short, very sharp knife blade and nip at the quill end, rather than saw at it, for best results.

During spring, when birds moult, look for a large wing feather with a strong shaft in a park or in your garden. Another idea is to ask the butcher at Christmas time for turkey or goose quills.

To make the writing point, cut diagonally across the end of the shaft and trim the cut end to make two inward-facing curves. Then nip off the tip, straight across, and cut a short vertical notch in the centre.

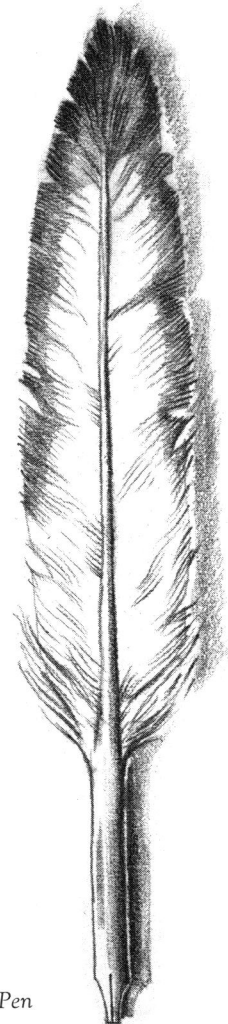

Quill Pen

Hiawatha Headpiece

INGREDIENTS

**strip of lightweight cardboard, approx. 10cm (4in)
wide, to fit around child's head
acrylic paints or felt-tip pens
feathers (seagull feathers are best)
craft glue
42 lengths of thick coloured wool,
each 15cm (6in) long
ribbon or leather thonging**

EQUIPMENT

**paintbrush
large stapler
scissors**

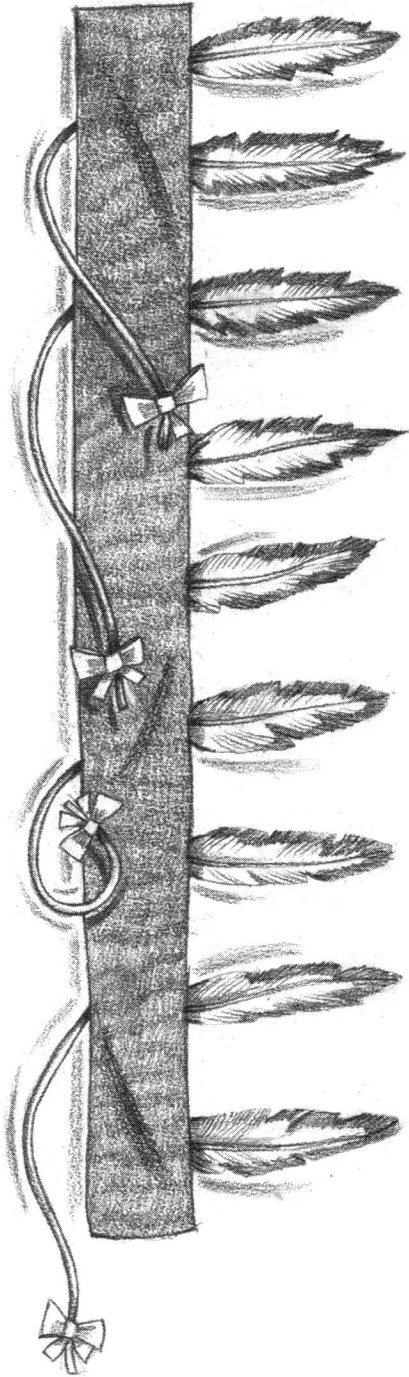

Fold the cardboard in half lengthwise and decorate one side with the paints or felt-tip pens.

Open the cardboard out and place it patterned side down. Glue the feathers firmly along the back of one side of the patterned cardboard. Allow the glue to dry and then staple the feathers if necessary. Refold the cardboard and glue the halves together firmly; this will keep the feathers in place.

Divide the lengths of wool into two bundles, then divide each bundle into three equal parts and plait the wool. Finish each plait with a ribbon bow or the leather thonging, and staple the plaits to the inside of the cardboard strip.

Fit the cardboard around the child's head and either glue or staple the edges to fit.

What better things to make with feathers than birds?

Egg -Bird

INGREDIENTS

selection of small feathers — flat ones for wings, soft downy ones for chest, longer ones for tail
blown egg (see p. 84)
craft glue
fuse wire
thin cardboard
medium-weight cardboard
yellow and black poster paints or felt-tip pens

EQUIPMENT
needle
scissors
paintbrush

Glue the feathers onto the bird's body (the egg), overlapping them in bands from the tail end and working towards the head, finishing with a collar of the smallest feathers. Depending on the size of the tail feathers, these can be glued at an angle to the base of the body, or wired into a fan shape.

Roll a small conical beak from the thin cardboard, paint it yellow and glue it on. Paint or draw black eyes. Cut two feet with tabs from the medium-weight cardboard and paint these yellow. Glue the tabs to the underside of the bird's belly, bending them back so that the bird will stand.

Seagull Marionette

This seagull will move its wings up and down, just like the real thing. Look for white and grey gull feathers when you are at the beach.

INGREDIENTS

spring-loaded wooden clothes peg
craft glue
white enamel paint
stiff white cardboard, 25cm (10in) square
feathers
plain typing paper
orange and black felt-tip pens
thick white sewing thread
2 pieces of thin dowelling or cane, 20cm (8in) long

EQUIPMENT
paintbrush
scissors
pencil
pin
sticky tape

Dismantle the clothes peg and set aside the wire part. Glue the two wooden pieces together lengthwise, with the notched sides facing each other. Paint the clothes peg white. This makes a nice body shape.

Cut the cardboard in half widthwise to make two pieces, each 12.5 x 25cm (5 x 10in). Draw an outline of a wing on each, putting the straight edge of the wing against the shorter side and taking it right out to the full width of the cardboard. Cut out both wings and decorate them with

feathers. Overlap the feathers like those on real wings. Leave the straight edge free. Glue the feathers in place.

Cut a strip of paper 1.5cm (½in) wide and about 6cm (2½in) long. Fold it in half so that the long sides meet and then fold again. Now cut it in half to make two hinges. Glue these hinges to the bottom sides of the wings and to the flat sides of the clothes peg behind the bird's 'head' (the top end of the clothes peg).

Make a small cardboard beak, colour it orange, and glue it to the bird's head. When the glue is dry, use the black felt-tip pen to draw the bird's two black legs folded up under the tail (on the underside of the clothes peg).

Cut two pieces of thread 60cm (2ft) long for the body. Cut another two pieces 75cm (2½ft) long for the wings. Tie one end of each of the shorter strings around the bird's head and before the tail starts. Tie the free end of each around each end of one of the pieces of dowelling. Use a pin to punch holes at each of the pointed ends of the wings and thread through the two longer lengths. Tie the free end of these to the other piece of the dowelling. Use sticky tape to secure the threads in place on the dowelling.

I wonder if it is a bird

That sings within the hidden tree,

Or some shy angel calling me

To follow far away.

GRACE H. CONKLING, 'NIGHTINGALES'

Bird Mobile

INGREDIENTS
heavy cardboard
felt-tip pens
selection of feathers, large and small
craft glue
string
2 pieces of thin dowelling, 30cm (12in) long
firm fuse wire
EQUIPMENT
pencil
scissors
hole punch

Draw six different-sized bird shapes on the thick cardboard and cut them out. Draw the birds' faces and beaks with the felt-tip pens, then glue feathers to both sides of each shape. Use the large or straight ones for the birds' wings, and the shorter, fluffier ones for their chests.

Use the hole punch to make a hole in the top of the body of each bird. Cut six different lengths of string and knot an end of each through the hole.

Wire the two pieces of dowelling together in the centre to form a cross. Tie a double length of string to the centre to hang the mobile. Tie the loose ends of the strings from the birds to the pieces of dowelling, adjusting the balance by moving the strings.

The Feather Game

This is fun with a group of players, or can be played by just two children. You need a piece of swansdown. The first player puffs it up in the air, and the other(s) must keep it aloft by blowing at it. If anyone lets it sink to the ground, they must pay a forfeit.

Old Mother Goose,

When she wanted to wander,

Would ride through the air

On a very fine gander.

SAND

My sons, Edward and Randall, love to build sandcastles — the bigger, the better. The trick to making really splendid sandcastles is preparation. Before you go to the beach, make some flags to put in the top of the castle turrets. Cut triangles out of thin cardboard and glue them to ice-block sticks. Decorate them with bright paints.

Take a shoe box to the beach with you to make good square-shaped walls. Take a small can, like a coffee can, as well as an ordinary bucket and spade — this makes a good shape for turrets. Another good idea is to take an old cooking funnel. Filled with damp sand and upended on top of the turrets, it makes a wonderful-looking spire on which to pop the flag.

But sand is not just for making castles.
Try some of these ideas:

Sand Sculptures

- Build a mountain of dampish sand and make grooves spiral around it. Race marbles down the grooves.
- Bury a friend or a grown-up in sand up to the neck. Shape the sand around their body into a rocket or a racing car.
- Make a zoo. Look for shells, seaweed and pebbles for animals and make fences from sticks.
- Right at the edge of the sea, where the sand is damp, build an enormous turtle or monster coming out of the sea. Mark out its eyes and fins with shells and seaweed.
- Play giant noughts-and-crosses. Use a stick to draw a board in the sand; round rocks can be the noughts and strips of sea weed can be the crosses.

To see a world in a grain of sand

And a heaven in a wild flower

Hold infinity in the palm

of your hand

And eternity in an hour.

William Blake, 'Auguries of Innocence'

(c. 1803)

I'm the king of the castle

And you're the dirty rascal!

Sand Painting

INGREDIENTS
½ cup silver sand
yellow, blue and green powder paints
piece of coloured lightweight cardboard,
25 x 30cm (10 x 12in)
white glue
EQUIPMENT
3 plastic containers
fork
pencil

Divide the sand equally between the three containers. Add a tablespoon or so of the different powder paints to each portion, mixing with the fork till you get the intensity of colour you want.

Pencil in a pattern or picture on the cardboard, and fill it in with the glue. Sprinkle thickly with the coloured sands and allow to dry.

Variation: Another idea is to put a sheet of drawing paper over the sand drawing and draw on the paper with wax crayons. The grainy texture of the sand underneath will come through on the drawing.

Coloured Sand Streams

INGREDIENTS
dry sand (sufficient to fill the jar)
food colouring
clear glass jar and non-metallic lid (an
old coffee jar is ideal)
EQUIPMENT
small plastic bags
baking sheets
funnel

Divide the sand into four or five portions and place each portion into a different plastic bag. Add different food colourings to each, a drop at a time, until you have the colour you require. (Colours like red, blue and green will colour the sand quite quickly. With yellow or orange, you might need more colouring to tint the sand.) Holding the top of the bags tightly closed, shake the bags well to mix the colour thoroughly through the sand.

Spread the coloured sand on baking sheets, keeping the colours separate. Place in a slow oven for 15–30 minutes to dry thoroughly, then allow to cool at room temperature for a further 30 minutes.

Using the funnel, pour a layer of one coloured sand into the jar, making little ripples and mounds as you do, especially around the walls. Then carefully pour a contrasting coloured sand over the top, accentuating the wavy shapes. Repeat, using all the different colours, all the way up the jar. Cap securely and use as a decoration or paperweight.

Apples and quinces,

Lemons and oranges,

Plump unpecked cherries,

Melons and raspberries,

Bloom-down-cheeked peaches,

Swart-headed mulberries,

Wild free-born cranberries,

Crab-apples, dewberries,

Pine-apples, blackberries,

Apricots, strawberries;

All ripe together

In summer weather ...

CHRISTINA ROSSETTI, 'GOBLIN MARKET' (1862)

Chapter Two

FRUIT AND VEGETABLES

There are many more things to do with fruit and vegetables than just eat them. They can be dried to make weird and wonderful shapes and puppets, or used to make stamps for printing, or even to make jewellery. And, because they do taste so good, there are also a few different cooking ideas in this section, like making Candied Apples! (With any projects that involve the use of the stove, it's a good idea for adults to supervise.)

Candied Apples

INGREDIENTS
4 small red or green apples
ice-block sticks
375g (12oz) packet of soft plain caramel
sweets
EQUIPMENT
double boiler
metal spoon
greaseproof paper

Wash and dry the apples. Push an ice-block stick into the base of each one and leave, upended, until the caramel is ready.

To make the caramel coating, place the caramels in the double boiler over gently simmering water and allow them to melt slowly, stirring with the metal spoon. Do not take your eyes off them or they will burn.

When the caramel mixture is sticky and liquid, dip the apples into it, one at a time, twirling by the stick to cover the apple thoroughly. Place the candied apples, upended, on a piece of greaseproof paper and allow to harden.

Variation: It is fun to decorate the apples while the caramel is still sticky. Make faces with chocolate drops for hair, licorice straps for eyebrows and moustaches, and jelly beans for eyes, nose and mouth.

Sugar Plums

These are an old-fashioned Christmas tree decoration — and they make a nice sweet at any other time too.

INGREDIENTS
500g (1lb) prunes, stones removed
500g (1lb) icing sugar
tulle or netting, cut into 12.5cm (5in)
squares
fine ribbon or gold string
EQUIPMENT
steamer
large plate or tray
baking tray or shallow-sided container
plastic cling wrap

Steam the prunes for 1 hour, or until they have plumped up well. Drain and set aside till cool.

Scatter icing sugar thickly on the large plate or tray and roll each prune in it two or three times till thickly coated. Place the prunes on the baking tray and cover with the cling wrap. Set aside and leave to cool and set overnight.

Wrap each 'sugar plum' in a tulle or netting square, tie the ends together with a piece of ribbon or string, and hang the sugar plums from the tree.

Orange Pomander

INGREDIENTS
**medium orange
cloves
orris root powder
cinnamon powder
net fabric
ribbon, 2cm (¾in) wide
dried flowers and cinnamon stick
(optional)
craft glue**
EQUIPMENT
**toothpick or skewer
mixing bowl
greaseproof paper**

Use the toothpick or a skewer to make holes for the cloves all over the skin of the orange. Insert the cloves, leaving a cross-shaped space where the ribbon will go around the fruit.

In the bowl, mix together roughly equal quantities of orris root powder and cinnamon powder. Roll the orange in this mixture, making sure it is well covered.

Wrap the orange in a piece of greaseproof paper and leave it to dry for 4 weeks in a dark, dry place. By then, you should have a small, dried-out pomander with a lovely citrus smell.

You can hang the pomander in a little net bag tied with a ribbon. If it is to be a present, glue on a cluster of dried flowers and a cinnamon stick to make it look really pretty.

Raspberry Ink

Use this special pale pink raspberry 'ink' to write messages or private poems in your diary. Raspberry juice can stain, so wear old clothes when you are mashing them in case they squirt up at you.

INGREDIENTS
2 tablespoons squishy, overripe raspberries
EQUIPMENT
**small glass jar
fork
very fine, non-metallic sieve
mapping pen**

Put the raspberries in the glass jar and mash them thoroughly with the fork. Add a little bit of water, and mash again. (The more water you add, the paler the ink you make will be.)

When you have reached the right consistency and colour strength, pour the ink through the sieve. Strain again to get rid of any tiny bits of seed or hairs.

Use the mapping pen to dip into the ink and write with.

The fun thing about making jewellery from fruit is that you can nibble on it as you work!

Cherry Earrings

Select pairs of cherries that are joined together at the top. Hang them over the tops of your ears so that one cherry dangles in front and one behind. If you want to, you can hang another pair around the front cherry and another round the back one, and so on, to create a really long chain. Nip the two stalks together with a tiny bit of thread so that they don't slip off.

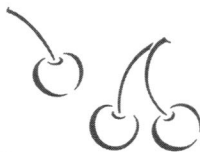

Blueberry Necklace

INGREDIENTS
punnet of firm blueberries (ripe ones will drip too much juice)
1½ cups small round macaroni
thread
EQUIPMENT
needle

Thread the needle and tie a knot. Thread on a blueberry, then a small piece of macaroni, then another blueberry, then another small piece of macaroni and so on, until you have the length you want for a necklace. Knot both ends together.

Popcorn Jewellery

INGREDIENTS
2 cups popping corn
shirring elastic
EQUIPMENT
needle

Pop the corn and set it aside to cool. Thread the needle with shirring elastic, tie a knot in one end and thread pieces of popcorn on to make a necklace, bracelet or anklet. When you have the right length of popcorn for your project, tie the ends together in a firm knot.

Carrot Necklace

INGREDIENTS
3 large carrots
thread
EQUIPMENT
needle
absorbent paper
drying rack

First, peel the carrots and cut them into slices. Thread the needle and tie a knot, leaving a length of thread to tie off the necklace with when you have finished making it.

Start by threading on small slices of carrot, then slightly larger ones till you reach the middle of the necklace —

approximately 30cm (12in) — then start threading on slightly smaller ones again, until you have two reasonably similar sides. Tie off the necklace and place it on absorbent paper on a drying rack.

Put the rack in a warm, dry place to dry the necklace out completely. This will take at least a fortnight. Then the necklace will be ready to wear.

Corn Dollies

In Europe and England corn dollies were once used in many ceremonies to do with harvesting crops. They were thought to be very lucky in ensuring plenty of food for the people of the particular tribe.

For this project, you will need to save the husks or outside leaves from fresh corn. About 12 should be right. You will also need some bright red cord.

Gather all the husks tightly together at one end, so that the ends are even, and tie tightly with a piece of the red cord. Make a second tie about 4cm (1½ in) down — this makes the head. Now separate about three strands to the left and three to the right, and tie the ends of these as 'wrists' for the dolly. Tie the next piece of cord around her waist, then divide the remaining six husks, three to the left and three to the right, and tie the last two pieces of cord around her ankles.

Halloween Pumpkin

It is traditional to celebrate Halloween on the evening of 31 October by displaying a pumpkin 'lantern'.

INGREDIENTS
**pumpkin
felt-tip pen or pencil
piece of oil cloth or flat china saucer
short candle**
EQUIPMENT
sharp knife

First buy — or grow — a very big yellow pumpkin, preferably with some stem remaining to act as a handle for the eventual lid. The best variety is Big Mac, which bears huge golden fruit up to 90cm (3ft) in circumference!

Using the felt-tip pen or pencil, draw a face on the pumpkin. Cut a circle around the stem with the sharp knife to form a lid, lift off and proceed to scoop out the contents, leaving the shell 2–2.5cm (^{3}/4–1in) thick. Cut out the face, using short, sharp strokes.

Take the candle (which should be short so that it won't scorch the lid), soften its base with a match and set it securely on the small piece of oil cloth or the flat china saucer. This sits on the base of the shell.

Place the lantern in the window so that everyone can see it on Halloween.

Variation: You can also use a large turnip for this project.

Halloween Pumpkin

Vegetables are the perfect raw materials for making strange and exotic creatures, because so many are oddly shaped to begin with. And if they aren't, you can make them so!

Square Tomatoes

What could be odder than a square tomato? Make the box from lightweight plastic.

INGREDIENTS
**clear plastic box, 4cm (1^1/2in) square
(from a gift shop or craft supplier)
adjustable craft knife
tomato plant bearing still-green tomatoes
craft glue or sticky tape
rubber band or string**

Cut out a small hole in the base of the plastic box to accommodate the stem of the tomato flower.

Secure the plastic box over a green tomato as it starts to grow inside the old flower, then glue or tape the lid of the box back on. Use the rubber band or string to loop around the box and tie it to the main stem of the tomato plant or the stake itself; otherwise the boxed tomato will sag and hurt the rest of the plant.

Once the tomato has grown to fill the whole box, carefully take off the lid and cut the tomato up in squares for sandwiches!

Gourd Painting

Gourds come in the most extraordinary range of shapes and sizes. Some have fat, spoon-shaped ends, others look like pears and others have long tube-like bodies that twist back on themselves like snakes. They are wonderful subjects to decorate in autumn, and to use to create a crazy collection of animals and gnomes.

First, wash and dry the gourd to remove any trace of dirt or mud. Look at the shape carefully — what does it suggest? Now, use oil-based paint to give it a zany personality.

Note for the grown-ups: Keep some mineral turps on hand for washing brushes and cleaning hands afterwards.

Vegetable Witch

The more you look at the shapes and colours of vegetables, the more ideas you will have for making people. A tomato cut in half, with the seeds scooped out, makes a great helmet. Celery sticks are perfect for arms and legs, while celery curls (made by slitting the ends and soaking in iced water in the fridge) are good for hairy eyebrows and bristly moustaches. Cabbage leaves are skirts or capes, slices of cucumber make chain mail for armour and oddly-shaped mushrooms and capsicums (sweet peppers) make weird pets for your vegetable person.

INGREDIENTS
large lumpy potato
small round potato
wooden toothpicks
brussels sprout
cabbage leaves
purple runner beans
small onion
medium carrot
baby carrot
shelled peas

Start with the large, lumpy potato — this will be the witch's body. Cut the smaller potato in half and use toothpick pieces to stick the halves to the bottom of the body as feet. The witch's apron is made from brussels sprout leaves and her cape from the cabbage leaves. Stick on two purple runner beans as speckly arms. The onion is her head.

To make the hair, peel the medium carrot into thin strips and stick them on. Cut the tip off the baby carrot and use this as a nose. Stick a row of peas all around the witch's shoulders as a magic necklace. Use two peas for the eyes.

Grumpy Apples

INGREDIENTS
2 large red apples
clear varnish
EQUIPMENT
vegetable peeler
adjustable craft knife
pins
baking sheet
cooling rack
paintbrush

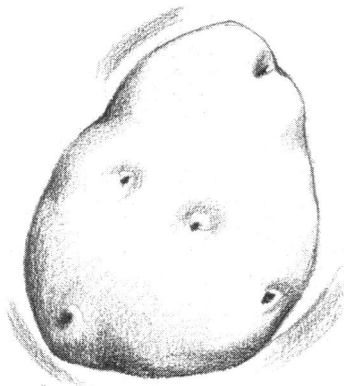

Use the vegetable peeler to peel the front half of the apple. Keep the strips of peel. Using the craft knife, carve out a chunky nose and a slit for the mouth. Cut two holes for the eyes. Cut pieces of peel to make eyebrows, a moustache, little square teeth, two eyes and so on. Press the features into place and secure with pins if necessary.

Preheat the oven to 60°C (140°F), place the apples on a baking sheet and bake for 1 hour. Cool on a rack and remove the pins. Leave in a warm, dry place to form grumpy, squished-up faces. When the Grumpy Apples are completely dry, paint them with clear varnish so they will keep.

Mr Potato

INGREDIENTS
large potato
small round radish
toothpicks, broken into small pieces
2 raisins
pointed end of carrot
slice of turnip

small piece of cottonwool, approx.
2.5cm (1in) square
seeds, e.g. alfalfa, cress

EQUIPMENT
penknife
nail scissors

Use the penknife carefully to cut the top off the potato, making a hollowed dent about 3cm (1¼in) deep in the centre. Cut a slice off the bottom so that it will stand up straight.

Cut two slices of radish and attach to Mr Potato with toothpick pieces as his eyes. Cap the tips of the toothpicks with raisins. Cut off the tip of the carrot and attach this as Mr Potato's nose. Using the nail scissors, cut two rectangular strips from the slice of turnip. Cut one edge of each strip in a zig-zag pattern — these will be his 'teeth'. Attach the turnip strips with toothpicks.

Wet and flatten the piece of cottonwool, place it in the hollow and sprinkle with the seeds. Pour some water into the hollow, and after a few days Mr Potato's 'hair' will sprout.

Cress Caterpillar

INGREDIENTS
7 baby potatoes
plastic toothpicks
matchsticks
2 tablespoons mustard and cress seeds
felt-tip pen

EQUIPMENT
bodkin or fine knitting needle
pump atomiser

Join the potatoes together with the plastic toothpicks to make the caterpillar's body. Use matchsticks for the legs, allowing for about four per potato. (It's also a good idea to make small holes with the knitting needle or bodkin where you want the legs to go first, otherwise the matchsticks might snap off.)

Make lots of little shallow holes all over the caterpillar's back and head with a toothpick. Push mustard and cress seeds into the holes. Spray the caterpillar lightly with water from the pump atomiser. There is no need to water it again, as there is enough water in the potatoes to sprout the mustard and cress.

Draw a face on the caterpillar's head with the felt-tip pen. Its 'hair' should sprout within a day or so!

Like leaves, some vegetables have the most surprisingly intricate and beautiful patterns. Think about the underside of a mushroom, for instance, all those feathery lines fanning out from the middle. Now, imagine what a lovely pattern of 'stars' you can make using a mushroom for printing with paint. Or a capsicum ...

Capsicum and Mushroom Prints

INGREDIENTS
medium capsicum (pepper)
large flat mushroom
poster paint
paper
EQUIPMENT
knife
tea-towel
saucer
newspaper

Cut the capsicum in half crosswise and remove the seeds. Set one half, cut-side down, on a tea-towel for 15 minutes to absorb excess moisture.

Dip the cut end into a saucer of paint, press lightly on newspaper to remove the excess, then press onto paper to print a pattern.

Now remove the stem from the mushroom and dip the underside into the saucer of paint. You need only a little paint or else you will lose the detail of the fine ridges.

The strong wiggly lines of the capsicum print make an interesting contrast to the soft starry shape of the mushroom print.

Variation: Instead of printing onto paper, print onto an old pillowcase or cushion cover. Or print onto a handkerchief and make it into a sachet bag as a present.

Potato Prints

INGREDIENTS
2 potatoes
poster paints
card or art paper
EQUIPMENT
penknife
tea-towel
skewer
saucer
scrap paper or newspaper

Cut the potatoes in half and stand them, cut-side down, on a tea-towel for 15 minutes to absorb excess moisture.

With your skewer, scratch different patterns on the cut parts of the potatoes. Cross, fish and leaf designs will all look good, or even just two wavy lines — it's better to have a simple design. Use the penknife to scrape out the potato flesh around the design so that you get a raised surface.

Pour about a tablespoon of paint into a saucer and dip the potato halves into it. Press them lightly onto a sheet of scrap paper or newspaper to get rid of any excess paint, then press onto the card or art paper.

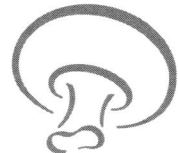

Apple Bobbing

This game is a great favourite in America at Halloween as well as at Christmas.

To play, fill a large (and steady) basin with water and float about a dozen apples in it. Players bend over the basin one at a time with their hands clasped or tied behind their backs, and try to pick up the apples with their teeth. Depending on the number and age of the players, a baby's bathtub might be a good option. Unless players are happy to get wet, tie tea-towels or bibs around their necks.

Variation: Another idea is to tie the apples to the clothes line with string. The players have to keep their hands behind their backs as they try to bite the apples.

Pass the Orange

This is a very old game which has passed the test of time. 'Pass the Orange' was played a lot in Victorian families — it is said that it was a particular favourite of couples who were in love!

Divide everyone into two teams and give each of the leaders a large, firm orange. They place the orange under their chin, wedge it firmly into position and clasp their hands behind their backs. They then have to pass it to the next player's chin and so on. The team that gets their orange from front to back first, wins.

Hickety Pickety
my black hen,
She lays eggs
for gentlemen
Sometimes nine and
sometimes ten . . .
Hickety, Pickety,
my black hen.

Chapter Three

EGGS

Humpty Dumpty sat on a wall,
Humpty Dumpty had a great fall.
All the King's horses and all the King's men
Couldn't put Humpty together again.

Decorated eggs are probably best known as a traditional Easter craft, eggs being a religious symbol of rebirth and a new beginning. Eggs can also be used year-round to make all sorts of other appealing natural crafts. Think about the possibilities of making blown-egg Christmas ornaments and egg mosaics.

Painted Eggs

INGREDIENTS
**hard-boiled eggs
poster paints
scraps of colourful fabric or paper, ribbons and stickers
craft glue**
EQUIPMENT
fine-tipped paintbrush or cotton buds

Paint the eggs, either with a paintbrush or (for smaller children) by pressing the tip of a cotton bud in the paint and using this as a brush.

When the paint is dry, decorate with the other materials, then allow the glue to dry.

Arrange the eggs in a basket in the centre of the lunch table on Easter Sunday.

Marbled Eggs

INGREDIENTS
**hard-boiled eggs
different food colourings**
EQUIPMENT
**cotton cloth, approx. 18cm (7in) square
(old hankies are perfect)
rubber bands
eye-dropper**

Slightly wet the piece of cloth or hanky and wrap it loosely around an egg, securing at each end with rubber bands, Christmas cracker-style.

Drip several drops of the different food colourings onto the damp cloth or hanky. Twist it back and forth by holding

A hen is only an egg's way of

making another egg.

SAMUEL BUTLER, *THE WAY OF ALL FLESH*

the rubber bands, forcing the colours to smudge together. Wait for 2 minutes, then unwrap the egg and set it aside to dry.

Rinse out the cloth or hanky, wring it till just damp and repeat the process.

Tie-dyed Eggs

These are not really tie-dyed, but they look very similar!

INGREDIENTS
hard-boiled eggs
2 shades of food colouring
EQUIPMENT
2 small bowls
eye-dropper
scissors
masking tape

Fill the two bowls with water, and use the eye-dropper to add drops of food colouring to each until you have two shades of the same intensity. Dunk the hard-boiled eggs briefly into one bowl of coloured water, then allow them to dry.

Cut out shapes from the masking tape, such as little stars, moons, flowers, rabbits or just squiggles. Stick them on the eggs. Dunk the eggs into the other bowl of coloured water, then remove them and allow to dry.

When the eggs are quite dry, peel off the masking-tape shapes — you should have a two-toned, 'tie-dyed' effect.

Batik Eggs

INGREDIENTS
hard-boiled eggs
white wax candle, sharpened to a point
food colouring
EQUIPMENT
small bowl

Draw a design or initials on the eggs with the wax, pressing firmly to get an even, thick line. Add food colouring to a small bowl of water, dunk the eggs into the water, then carefully lift them out and allow to dry.

Onion Skin Eggs

INGREDIENTS
4 eggs
2 brown-skinned onions
EQUIPMENT
old pantyhose or stocking foot
saucepan
slotted spoon
old tea-towel or newspaper

Peel the onions. Chop the brown outer skins roughly and place them in the stocking foot. Knot to secure.

Bring a saucepan of water to the boil and put in the onion bag. Reduce the heat and simmer for 25 minutes. Add the eggs gently, so as not to crack them, and cook for 5–7 minutes.

Remove the eggs with the slotted spoon and allow to dry on the old tea-towel or newspaper.

Glamorous Glitter Eggs

INGREDIENTS
2 hard-boiled eggs
double-sided sticky tape
pink or purple ribbon, approx. 1.5cm
(½in) wide and 30cm (12in) long
craft glue
rainbow glitter
EQUIPMENT
scissors
2 eggcups
glue brush or soft paintbrush

Boil the eggs for 10 minutes, set aside and allow to cool completely. Run a piece of double-sided sticky tape around the middle of each egg. Cut a piece of the decorative ribbon to fit around each egg and press it carefully over the double-sided tape.

Place the eggs in the eggcups, brush the top halves with glue and sprinkle generously with glitter. When the top halves are dry, invert the eggs and glue glitter to the bottom halves.

Blown Eggs

INGREDIENTS
eggs
thread
EQUIPMENT
fine needle
bowl

Pierce the pointed end of an egg with the needle, then make a slightly larger hole in the flatter end. Let the white and yolk run out into a bowl, rinse the shell carefully and allow it to dry.

Decorate the shell any way you like.

Egg Ornaments

INGREDIENTS
blown eggs (see above)
poster paints or felt-tip pens
glitter
clear varnish
thread
glitter string or narrow satin ribbon,
approx. 3mm (⅛in) wide
EQUIPMENT
very long sewing needle or bodkin
eggcups
craft glue
paintbrush

Stand each blown egg in an eggcup to decorate. Use the poster paints or felt-tip pens to create a bright pattern — stars or dots or a zigzag — and finish off with glitter.

Carefully paint all over the egg with the clear varnish and leave it to dry completely.

Thread the needle or bodkin. Put the needle very carefully through the tiny hole at the top of the eggshell, and gently and slowly pull the thread all the way through the shell and out the other, wider end. Remove the needle. Tie a knot in the thread to secure the shell to the thread. Tie the thread to a loop of glitter string or narrow ribbon.

Egg Houses

INGREDIENTS
blown eggs (see opposite)
felt-tip pens
thin cardboard
poster paints
craft glue
reusable adhesive, e.g. Blu-Tack
medium-weight cardboard
pebbles, twigs
small flat mirror
EQUIPMENT
scissors
paintbrush

Draw windows and doors on the eggs with the felt-tip pens. Make little roofs for the egg houses by cutting rectangles out of the thin cardboard, painting different-coloured tiles on them and folding them in half. Glue them into place on top of the eggs.

Arrange the eggs as a little village, using the reusable adhesive to fix them to the medium-weight cardboard. Put paths made from pebbles between the houses, and put trees made from twigs in their gardens. The mirror can be a pond in the middle of the village.

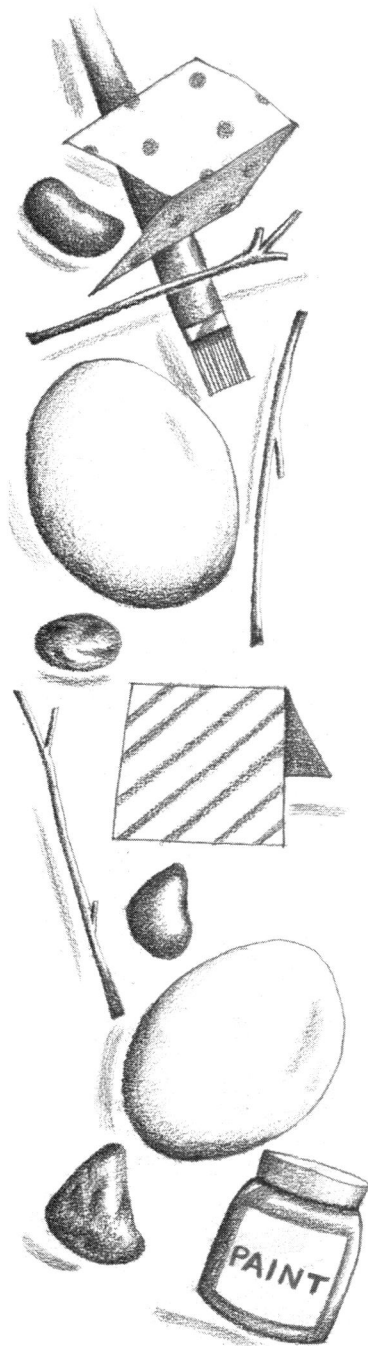

Making Egg Houses

Elizabeth, Elspeth, Betsy and Bess

They all went together to seek a

bird's nest;

They found a bird's nest with five

eggs in it.

They all took one and left four in it.

Egg People

INGREDIENTS
4 eggs
poster paints
felt-tip pens
potting mix
cress seeds
EQUIPMENT
adjustable craft knife
4 eggcups
reusable adhesive, e.g. Blu-Tack, or modelling clay
paintbrush

Soft-boil the eggs and then, using the adjustable craft knife, very carefully cut the top off each, in as straight a line as possible. Scoop out the eggs (eat them if you like!) and rinse out the shells.

When dry, secure each eggshell half in an eggcup with a dab of reusable adhesive and paint on faces with the felt-tip pens and poster paints. Make them all different faces — perhaps one with freckles, one with glasses and one with a beard.

Carefully fill each eggshell with potting mix and sprinkle with cress seed, pushing the seeds just beneath the surface of the mix. Water very lightly so as not to streak the painted faces on the front of the shells — just enough to moisten the soil is fine — then sprinkle with water every day or so. Wait for the 'hair' to sprout from the Egg People's heads.

Painted eggshell pieces were used to make mosaics and to decorate pots and boxes many hundreds of years ago. Very old examples of this craft have been found by archaeologists and kept in museums. Eggshells will last a long time if prepared and used correctly.

Eggshell Flower Pots

INGREDIENTS
**6 eggs
poster paints
small plastic plant pot, approx.
9cm (3½in) diameter
clear silicon glue
clear spray varnish**
EQUIPMENT
**old tea-towel
paintbrush**

Hard boil the eggs and cool them. Peel off the shells, keeping the pieces as large as possible. Rinse the shells carefully and allow to dry on a tea-towel.

Paint the eggshell pieces with different-coloured poster paints and allow to dry. Break into different-sized pieces — small, medium and large.

Coat the plant pot with the glue and press the eggshell pieces onto it in a pattern — wavy stripes of the different colours look great. When the glue is quite dry, spray the pot with a coat of clear varnish.

Egg Mosaic

INGREDIENTS
**6 eggs
poster paints
drawing paper
stiff cardboard
wallpaper paste**
EQUIPMENT
**old tea-towel
2 small soft paintbrushes
pencil
plastic ice-cream container
tweezers**

Hard boil the eggs, cool them and peel off the shells in as large pieces as possible. (You can use the eggs to make an egg salad.) Rinse the shells carefully and allow them to dry on a tea-towel.

Paint the eggshell pieces with bright poster paints, and allow to dry thoroughly. Break the curved pieces of eggshell into small flat pieces.

In the meantime, sketch out a design on the drawing paper — perhaps a flower, or sun or star shape. Mount the drawing paper on the cardboard.

Make up a thick mixture of wallpaper paste in the ice-cream container and, using the other paintbrush, brush inside the sections of your design that are to be covered with the mosaic pieces. Use the tweezers to place the eggshell fragments on the wet pasted surface, working fairly quickly. Leave the mosaic to dry, and then hang it on the wall.

Jack and Jill went up the hill

To fetch a pail of water.

Jack fell down and broke his crown

And Jill came tumbling after.

Up Jack got and home did trot

As fast as he could caper.

He went to bed to mend his head

with vinegar and brown paper.

Chapter Four

PAPER AND CARDBOARD

It's not usually necessary to have to go out and buy pieces of cardboard and paper, though you might want something in a special colour for a project. Most homes have enough old cardboard cartons, scrap paper and newspaper to start their own recycling business! Always keep the nice pieces of birthday paper or Christmas paper that come your way too — they are terrific for colourful projects like the paper flowers.

Beautiful ornamental flowers can be made from paper and, once you have mastered the idea, from velvet, silk and even feathers. The simplest way to make lovely roses is to use crepe paper. The flowers need not be realistic — in fact, the more amazing and fantastic they are, the better.

Crepe Paper Flower

Crepe Paper Flowers

INGREDIENTS

crepe paper
cottonwool
green florist's tape
tiny pearl beads or leftover rhinestone chips,
for the stamens
fine fuse wire, for attaching the stamens
stronger fuse wire, for the stem
felt, satin or silver foil
craft glue

EQUIPMENT

scissors

First, make the centre of the flower by folding a piece of satin or crepe paper over a wad of cottonwool about 2.5cm (1in) around. Secure tightly with the florist's tape.

Wire the flower's stamens in place, tucking the ends of the fine fuse wire under the flower's centre and out of sight.

Attach short pieces of the fine fuse wire to the underside of the flower centre to act as a base for the stem. Twist these around a piece of the stronger fuse wire, which forms the stem.

Cut the petals out of crepe paper, using a heart shape, and wrap them, pointed end downmost, around the flower centre. Furl tightly in and around the flower centre at first, and then blouse the outer petals outwards, stretching the rim of the paper with your thumbs.

Secure the base of the flower petals with green florist's tape and then wrap the wired stem thickly with either felt, satin or foil. If using fabric, you will need to glue the stem covering in place.

Tissue Paper Flower

INGREDIENTS
tissue paper in six different colours
green and yellow pipe-cleaners
EQUIPMENT
saucer, approx. 12.5cm (5in) diameter
pencil
scissors
skewer

Put the sheets of tissue paper in a pile. Put the saucer face down on the sheets and trace around it. Cut out the circle, through all the layers.

Use the skewer to poke two holes next to each other at the centre of the layers. Push a yellow pipe-cleaner through one hole, bend it, and push it back through the other hole to form a centre. Twist the two ends together to form a stem, and wrap with a green pipe cleaner.

Fluff out the tissue paper petals, spreading them with your finger and thumb.

Cardboard Box Costume

INGREDIENTS
sturdy cardboard box, approx. 40 x 30cm
and 60cm high (16 x 12in
and 24in high)
poster paints or various found objects,
for decoration
ribbon or thick bias binding
craft glue
EQUIPMENT
knife
scissors
paintbrush
large stapler

Open the top flaps of the box. Turn the box over and cut an oval hole in the bottom that is large enough for you to fit into. Open out two of the side flaps. Paint the box and the flaps, or decorate by gluing on found objects.

Step into the box and hold it up under your arms. Ask an adult to measure lengths of ribbon or thick bias binding, and staple them over each shoulder, braces-style.

Sometimes you probably have more fun with cardboard boxes than you do with whatever came in them ...

Cardboard Box TV or Puppet Theatre

Cut off the top flaps of a cardboard box, then cut out a rectangle from one side. You can wear the box and be the 'announcer', or you can stage a puppet show, using the box as a theatre. See Chapter 7 for some ideas for puppets.

Silhouette

INGREDIENTS

sticky tape
sheet of black paper
sheet of white paper
craft glue

EQUIPMENT

torch
pencil
scissors

First, use the sticky tape to attach the sheet of black paper to a wall or cupboard.

Now sit on a chair so that the paper is right behind your head. Ask a grown-up to shine a torch at your profile and outline this profile with pencil on the black paper.

Cut out the profile and glue it to the white paper.

Whirligig

INGREDIENTS
white poster board
felt-tip pens or coloured pencils
screw-top bottle cap
pin
unsharpened pencil with rubber attached
sticky tape

EQUIPMENT
compass
pencil
scissors

Use the compass and pencil to draw a 12.5cm (5in) diameter circle on the cardboard. Cut the circle out and decorate it with the felt-tip pens or coloured pencils — a spiral or a star will look terrific when the whirligig gets going.

Cut six straight lines, equally spaced, towards the centre of the circle, stopping about 1.5cm (½in) before the centre point.

Make a tiny hole in the centre of the card circle and another in the centre of the bottle cap. Press the pin through the card, then through the bottle cap from the inside. Push the point of the pin into the rubber top of the pencil. Use the sticky tape to secure the back of the card circle to the cap.

Bend back wedges of the cardboard along the cut lines to form wing shapes — these will catch the wind and make the whirligig spin.

Take the whirligig outside on a breezy day and hold it while it spins.

Scrap Paper Spirals

This is a good way to learn about how hot air rises. Hold the spiral over a warm air current and it will spin around slowly; hold it in a cold spot and it will not move.

INGREDIENTS
light scrap card or stiff paper (old Christmas cards are just the right weight)
blue and yellow poster paints
thread
EQUIPMENT
scissors
paintbrush

Cut out a spiral from a square of the scrap card or paper. Colour one side blue and the other yellow. Hang the spiral by a thread with a knot at one end.

Scrapbook

This will give you somewhere to house your different collections — postcards, labels, phone cards, recipes, cards and pressed flowers, for example.

INGREDIENTS
heavy cardboard
adhesive paper
art paper
ribbon, leather thonging, raffia or string
EQUIPMENT
knife
scissors
hole punch

Take two pieces of heavy cardboard for the cover, using the knife to score 4cm (1½in) from one long side of each so that the book will open easily. Bend the cardboard pieces back on the scored lines and cover both smoothly with the adhesive paper.

Make an appropriate design for the cover — your initials can be pasted or painted on, for example.

Cut pieces of firm art paper 1.5cm (½in) smaller than the covers on three sides only (when the scrapbook is assembled, the sides of the pages with the holes in should be flush with the spine). Use the hole punch to make holes in the pieces of paper, then punch holes along the scored side of each cover at points to match.

Thread all the pieces together, using ribbon, leather thonging, bright raffia or string.

Paper Bag Bumble Bee

The only problem with this is making sure you don't pop all the bubble wrap before you get started!

INGREDIENTS
large brown-paper grocery bag
black and yellow poster paints
bubble wrap
sticky tape
EQUIPMENT
scissors
paintbrush
stapler

Cut a hole for your head in the bottom of the grocery bag, and another two oval arm holes in the narrower sides. Paint black and yellow stripes on the front of the bag.

To make the wings, scrunch up the bubble wrap in the middle and wrap sticky tape around it. Round off the wing edges with scissors. Tape or staple the wings to the back of the paper bag.

Paper Bag House

*One look at the bundles of newspapers
left outside houses on recycling
collection days is enough to show you
that it doesn't take long to save enough
paper for this project.*

INGREDIENTS
**24 large brown-paper grocery bags
about 20 old weekend newspapers
masking tape
old sheet or towels**

Fold over the top third of each bag and
crease. Now open out each bag and stuff it
with about 20 sheets of scrunched-up
newspaper until quite firm. Fold over the
top third along the creases, tuck in the
edges to make a block shape and tape the
top closed. Paint or decorate the blocks if
you wish.

To make a house, build three walls from
the blocks, taping them together with
masking tape. Drape a sheet or towels over
the top to make a roof.

Bird Whistles

*Many, many years ago, hunters would
cut whistles from thin pieces of bark.
Experiment with different thicknesses of
paper to make different-sounding
whistles — a thinner piece of paper will
make a deeper sound, while a thicker
one will make a higher note.*

Cut strips of paper approximately 7.5 x
2cm (3 x ¾in) and fold in half. Cut a V-
shaped notch in the fold. Turn up both free
ends about 1.5cm (½in) and crease.

To use, hold the whistle loosely
between two fingers close to the folds,
place the fold between your lips and
blow hard down against the notch. The air
will make the notch vibrate and create
different, strange sounds. Experiment
with different whistles and different-
shaped notches to make different bird or
animal sounds.

Paper Beads

INGREDIENTS
**drawing paper
wallpaper paste
poster paints
clear varnish
coloured yarn**
EQUIPMENT
**pencil
scissors
plastic bucket
greaseproof paper or old cake rack
paintbrush**

Use the pencil to mark out a square on the
paper and cut this into 12 rectangular
strips, each about 4 x 12.5cm (1½ x 5in).

Mix up the wallpaper paste in the

plastic bucket. Dunk each strip into the paste, wetting it on both sides. Wrap the strip smoothly and evenly around the pencil to form a bead, then slip it off and place on a piece of greaseproof paper or the cake rack to dry overnight. Repeat with the other strips.

When the beads are quite dry, paint them with bright poster paints and then add a coat of clear varnish. Thread them onto the yarn and tie the ends together.

Making papier-mâché is fun, although it can be messy. You will need lots of newspaper, both to make the papier-mâché, and to put down on the floor or table surface where you are working. You will also need to work fairly quickly, when covering the Piggy Bank or Pinata described here, so that the wallpaper paste does not thicken up too much.

Papier-mâché Piggy Bank

INGREDIENTS
balloon
old newspapers
wallpaper paste
opaque white paint
poster paints
corks, wire, dried beans, bottle caps,
pipe-cleaners or carpet remnants
clear spray varnish
EQUIPMENT
2 buckets
wooden spoon

Making Papier-mâché for Pinatas

INGREDIENTS
old newspapers
wallpaper paste
balloon
EQUIPMENT
2 plastic buckets
wooden spoon
small bowl
paintbrush

Cover a work surface with a few sheets of newspaper. Mix the wallpaper paste with water in one bucket, according to the instructions on the packet, and let it stand for 15 minutes.

Meanwhile, tear up a dozen or so sheets of newspaper into thin strips. Place them in the other bucket.

Blow up the balloon and tie a knot to secure. Sit the balloon in the small bowl so that it will stay still to work on.

Stir the paste and start dipping the strips of newspaper into the paste, then stick them all over the balloon, except around the knotted end. Smooth them out with your hands. After two or three layers of newspaper strips have been applied, brush over the shape with extra wallpaper paste and leave it to dry overnight.

The next day you can burst the balloon and remove the pieces.

small bowl
paintbrush
knife

Coat the balloon with papier-mâché using the method described on page 97. The only difference is that you don't have to leave a space around the knotted end. When the balloon shape is quite dry, cut a slot in the piggy's stomach or back with a pointed knife. Pull out the pieces of burst balloon.

Apply a coat of opaque white paint, then decorate with bright poster colours. Either paint on the piggy's ears, eyes and tail, or make them with materials such as corks, wire, dried beans, bottle caps, pipe-cleaners or even remnants of carpeting.

Once dry, the painted parts of the piggy bank can be sprayed with clear varnish.

Birthday Pinatas

In Mexico, when a child has a birthday, it is traditional to hang big papier-mâché parcels filled with surprises and sweets from the ceiling. The children are then blindfolded and given a stick, which they use to hit the pinatas and break them open. If it is a party, and it's warm, hang them outside on the clothes line or from tree branches. Fill one with sweets, one

with dried peas, one with scraps of paper, one with paper hats and whistles, and so on.

INGREDIENTS
large balloons
cooking oil
wallpaper paste
strips of newspaper
wrapped sweets
string
poster paints
EQUIPMENT
2 buckets
wooden spoon
small bowl
paintbrush

Blow up the balloons and knot or tie them. Paint the balloons with oil, then cover them with papier-mâché strips (see method on page 97), remembering to leave a space around the knotted ends. Leave the balloons for one whole day and night to dry completely.

Burst the balloons and pull the pieces out. Fill each pinata with sweets, put in one end of a piece of string with a large knot tied in it, then paste a layer of papier-mâché strips over the opening, thus securing the string in place. Dab extra paste around the base of the string if necessary. Set aside to dry. When the pinatas are dry, paint them with bright colours.

Chapter Five

RECYCLED TREASURE

Girls and boys come out to play

The moon is shining bright as day

Leave your supper and leave your sleep

And join your playfellows in the street;

Come with a hoop, come with a call,

Come and be merry, or not at all

Rather than contribute to the ever-increasing problem of landfills, I use up everything from plastic bottles to old tyres and old clothes to make something interesting and practical — given a little imagination. I never throw anything out without asking my sons if they want it. Invariably they do, and if they don't, the school or daycare centre love 'treasures' like these.

Can Stilts

A pair of can stilts are quick and easy to make and provide plenty of fun.

INGREDIENTS
2 large steel cans (not aluminium)
acrylic paints
2 pieces of thick string, each 120cm (4ft) long
EQUIPMENT
paintbrush
hammer and nail, or awl
metal file

Select cans that are the same height and of a width that a child can comfortably stand upon. Wash the cans and remove any labels, then decorate them with acrylic paints — numbers, zigzags, or the child's initials are all good ideas.

When the paint is dry, make two holes opposite each other near the outside edge at the closed end of each can, using either the awl or the hammer and nail. Finish the holes' edges with a metal file to ensure they will not fray the strings.

Thread a piece of thick string through the holes in each can and join the two ends with a reef knot. This means the length of the strings can be adjusted to suit each user, just by shifting the knot.

Tyre Swing

Every child dreams about being able to fly! And an old car tyre is probably the best choice for a swing if you have small children, as it is so much safer than a wooden seat if pushed without an occupant, and it's easier to hang on to.

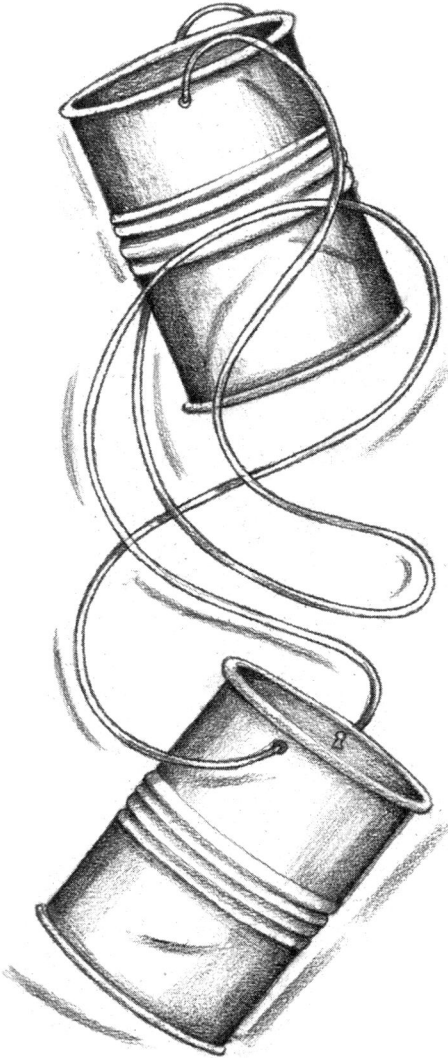

**steel eye bolt and 2 galvanised washers
nylon rope or chain, 2cm (¾in) thick
old car tyre**
EQUIPMENT
electric drill

For safety reasons, it's advisable to either hang or build your swing over grass or sand, rather than concrete. Position the rope so that even at full swing there's no risk of hitting another object, such as a wall or the tree itself.

Keep the area in front of the swing clear for children to jump when getting off.

The most important thing to remember about a tyre swing is to avoid tying the free end of the rope or chain directly around a branch. It is easy to knot a rope or chain around a branch but there is a very real risk that this could cause the branch to ringbark itself and weaken or even cause a welt that will let in infection and possibly kill the whole tree. It is far better to drill a hole right through the branch and then insert a big steel eye bolt, ring side downmost, securing it snugly at the top and bottom with galvanised washers. To ensure the washers are really firm against the branch, you may have to chisel away a little of the surrounding bark and then screw the washers right up into the wood. Again, though it sounds surprising, this is less likely to cause any harm to the tree and will, in fact, reduce the likelihood of infection.

Once the bolt is secure, it's simply a matter of hanging the tyre itself. The length of rope you will need will obviously vary. However, you should aim to have the bottom edge of the tyre no lower than 60cm (2ft) off the ground. Never use clothes line or other cheap rope for a tyre swing. Fine chain or strong nylon rope, at least 2cm (¾in) thick, is necessary for safety's sake. Be sure to check the rope from time to time, especially where it is tied to the tyre, to watch for fraying.

I remember, I remember,

Where I was used to swing;

And thought the air must rush

as fresh

To swallows on the wing;

My spirit flew in feathers then ...

And summer pools could

hardly cool

The fever on my brow!

THOMAS HOOD, 'I REMEMBER' (1826)

Tyre Garden Bed

If there's an old unroadworthy spare tyre in the garage, why not recycle it as a raised garden bed? Place the tyre flat on the ground and fill it with soil, then plant it with bulbs, flowers, seedling vegetables like baby carrots, or herbs.

This is a good method for growing plants that need special types of soil that is different from the rest of the garden — for instance, you could make a very sandy mix and create a miniature cactus garden in the raised tyre bed.

Tyre Tread Shoes

One very fashionable American shoe company has started making sandals out of recycled tyres, with only one drawback — they're very expensive! It's not hard to copy their idea, and make your own.

INGREDIENTS
old car tyre
**inner tube from car tyre,
or one from bike tyre**
carpet tacks
EQUIPMENT
chalk
**adjustable craft knife
or fine-tooth saw**
hammer

Using chalk, mark out the soles of the shoes on the tyre, using your right foot and then left as a guide. Cut out the soles, using the craft knife or the fine-tooth saw. Cut four strips from the inner tube rubber, each about 4cm (1½in) wide.

Put your right foot on the right sole, tread-side down, and place two strips of inner tube over the top of your foot so that they hold your foot onto the sole snugly. Mark the spot on the inner tube, take your foot out, and nail the inner-tube strips to the sides of the sole with the carpet tacks. Repeat with the left foot.

Bird Feeder Tray

If you'd like to try making a bird feeder as a project, start with something very simple. A platform made from an old off-cut of external housing timber or a scrap of plywood can easily be turned into a feeding tray. Sand off any rough edges (birds can get splinters just as easily as humans can!), and tack a beading edge around the tray to stop all the seed going straight onto the ground below.

A nice idea is to attach the feeder beneath a windowsill where you can all watch from inside. Use masonry bolts or galvanised nails if the house is made from timber.

The placement of the feeder is most important. And remember that birds, like children, are creatures of habit, so once you have found a spot they like, leave the feeder there. Another point worth remembering is to hang the feeder where it will not be exposed to strong winds. (This is especially the case with purchased hanging feeders — no self-respecting bird is going to enjoy clinging to a feeder that swings about wildly in the breeze.) Also, pick a spot that receives plenty of sun year-round for feeders.

There's something very satisfying about string. You can do so much with it too — it's not just for tying knots!

Rope Donkey

INGREDIENTS
**rope or thick coarse string
fine wool
scraps of wool and felt
craft glue**
EQUIPMENT
scissors

Cut nine lengths of rope or string, each about 60cm (2ft) long. Tie three together at one end and plait, tying off the top and bottom of the plait with fine wool. Repeat with another set of three pieces of rope or string.

Plait the other three lengths of rope differently. Plait the middle only, leaving about 7.5cm (3in) free at both ends. At one of the ends, fan out the strands of rope, then divide the strands in half. Plait two small thick plaits — these will be the donkey's ears. The other

Making a Birdbath

Birds need water every day in order to survive. Apart from drinking, birds also need water to take a bath in. So, to attract them to your garden in the first place, ensure there is a birdbath.

You can easily make a homemade birdbath. An old garbage-tin lid mounted on a terracotta drainage pipe with a small rock suspended on a rope down the middle as a 'plumb' to steady the lid makes a quite acceptable-looking birdbath. Simplest of all is a rock with a natural dent in it, or a ceramic saucer placed on a tree stump out of reach of predators.

You will find that once birds have been attracted to your place by water, they will want to stay and look for something to eat.

Birdbath

unplaited end will be its tail. Bend back the fat part of this plait to make the donkey's head and tie with the fine wool.

Hold the three plaits together in the middle and tie with wool. Make a saddle out of a square of felt or wool and wrap it around the middle of the donkey. Glue underneath. Bend the donkey's legs down so that it stands, and move its head upwards.

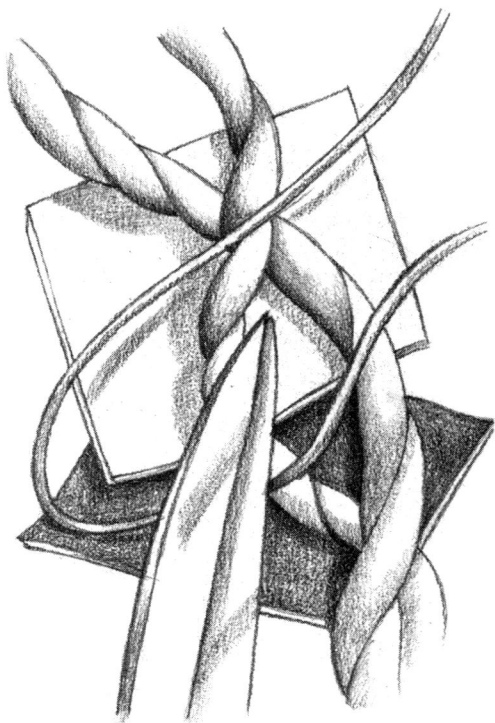

Materials needed for making a Rope Donkey

String Printing

INGREDIENTS
medium-weight cardboard
craft glue or glue-stick
different types of string, e.g. hessian,
wool, rope, raffia
poster paint
paper
EQUIPMENT
pencil
paint tray or aluminium foil tray
2 paint rollers

Sketch an outline of a swirling, curving pattern on the cardboard. Run glue along the outline, a little at a time, and stick down the string as you go. Tie knots in the different pieces of string to create a contrasting effect. When you have glued down all the different pieces of string, set the cardboard aside to dry.

Pour thick poster paint into the paint tray or aluminium foil tray. Cover one roller thickly and run over the top of the string picture several times, ensuring the whole picture is thickly and evenly coated with paint.

Place the paper over the top of the string picture and press down, using the dry roller to smooth the paper gently if the string design is very thick and uneven.

Variation: Use very large pieces of butcher's paper or brown paper, and repeat the string picture design 4–6 times, to make a large piece of wrapping paper.

Egg Carton Bells

With this idea, you can either make a string of the bells, or hang each one by itself — they look really pretty at Christmas.

INGREDIENTS
**egg carton
silver foil
craft glue
glitter
silver string or coloured raffia**
EQUIPMENT
**scissors
paintbrush
thick needle or bodkin**

Cut out the 12 individual cups from the egg carton. Cut out pieces of foil, each about 10cm (4in) square.

Glue the back of each square and wrap it around each cup, tucking the ends up inside. Paint the outside of each foil-covered cup with glue and sprinkle with glitter.

Use the thick needle or bodkin to punch a small hole in the top of each egg cup. Thread the silver string or coloured raffia through the holes, tying knots between each bell. Alternatively, hang each one separately, leaving a 'tongue' of string or raffia, and attaching a small 'clapper' made by crushing a little piece of foil into a tiny round ball.

All kids love to make a noise, and it might as well be as tuneful as possible! A group of children could each make a different instrument and put on a concert.

Lagerphone

Some country bands include a lagerphone, and the person playing it always seems to be having great fun, thumping away.

INGREDIENTS
**2 pieces of wood, one 12.5 x 60cm (5 x 60in), the other 12.5 x 30cm (5 x 30in)
red gloss paint
nails
80–100 metal bottle caps
ribbons**
EQUIPMENT
**sandpaper
paintbrush
hammer**

Sand the two pieces of wood, then paint them. Allow them to dry. Nail the two pieces of wood together to form a cross.

Nail in the bottle caps in rows up the cross and out to the sides. Do not hammer the nails right in, only about halfway so that the bottle caps can rattle around.

Tie the ribbons together in a large clump and nail it to the top of the lagerphone for a colourful effect.

To play your lagerphone, bang it up and down, or run a stick or piece of metal up and down the caps.

Saucepan Lid Cymbals

INGREDIENTS

**2 old aluminium saucepan lids (or metal lids
from a biscuit tin)
leather thonging or thick ribbon**
EQUIPMENT
hammer and awl

Use the hammer and awl to make two holes in the middle of each of the lids. Thread a length of leather thonging or thick ribbon through the holes and tie to make a loop.

Of course, if the lids still have their handles, they can be crashed together without any preparation.

Toilet Roll Flute

INGREDIENTS
**old toilet roll tube
greaseproof paper**
EQUIPMENT
**skewer
pencil**

Use a skewer and then a pencil to make a series of holes along one side of the tube. Cut out a circle of greaseproof paper and secure it firmly over one end of the tube with a rubber band.

Hum into the other open end, while you move your fingers over the holes to create different sounds.

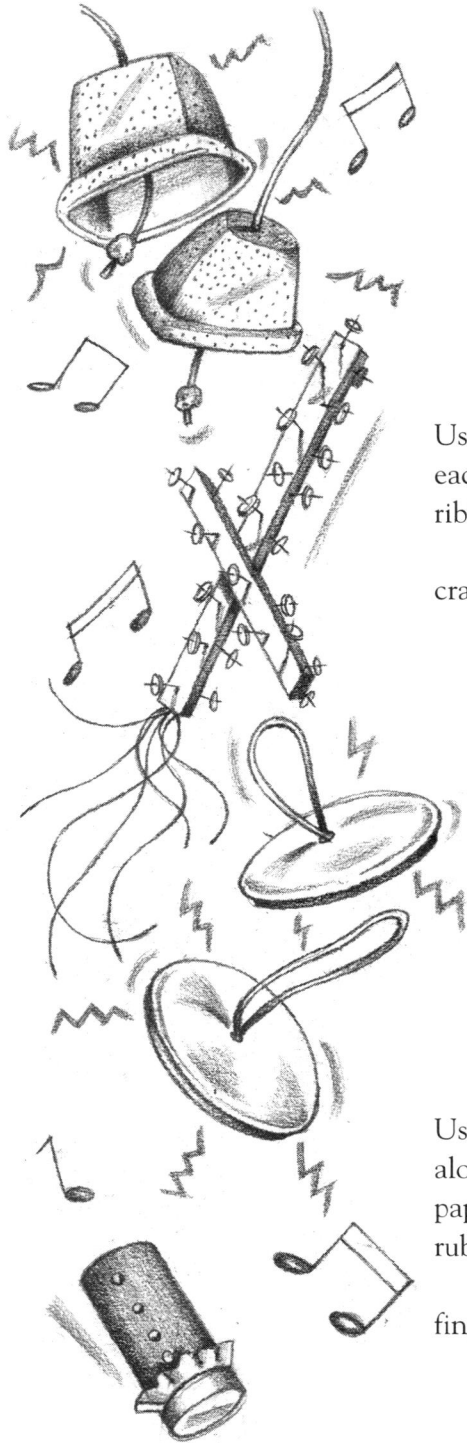

Bottle Organ

If you are putting on a show, tint the water in the bottles different colours with food colouring. You could even try having two rows of bottles, one for the right hand and one for the left.

INGREDIENTS
**9 glass bottles of varying sizes, e.g. jam jars,
milk bottles, wine bottles
water
wooden and metal skewers**

Stand the bottles in a row and fill each with water to a different level. You will find that each one 'plays' a different note when you strike it lightly with a skewer. (You will also find that metal and wooden skewers give you different sounds.) Run the skewer lightly along the bottles, as if you were playing a xylophone.

Comb Harmonica

One of the first memories I have of my father is of him teaching me to make a comb to hum. Fold a piece of greaseproof paper over a comb, press it to your lips and hum.

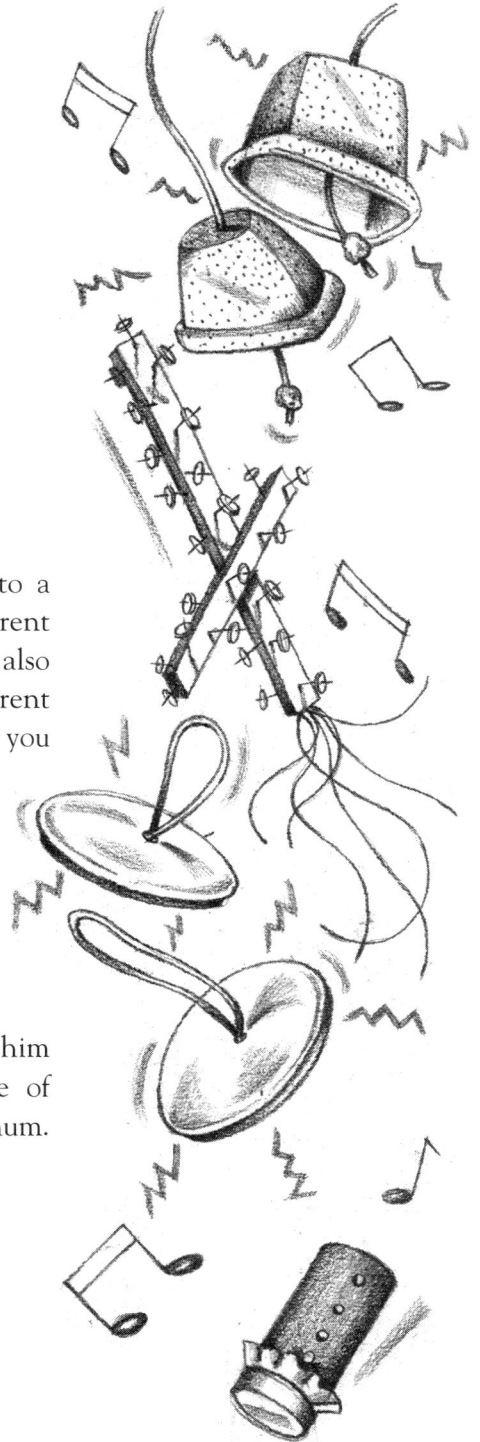

Cork-rimmed Hat

Australian drovers sometimes wore hats like these. The corks helped to shoo away the ever-present flies.

INGREDIENTS
string
about 20 corks
wide-brimmed hat
EQUIPMENT
scissors
skewer
large-eyed needle

Cut the string into 20 lengths, each about 25cm (10in) long. Use the skewer to make a hole, lengthwise, in each of the corks.

Thread the needle with the first piece of string and pass it first through the brim of the hat and then through the cork. Tie the ends together. Repeat with the rest of the corks all around the hat.

Jeans Tail

A tail is a great thing to have. Once you've had one for a while, walking and sitting with it feels quite normal. In fact, it actually doesn't feel right without it...

INGREDIENTS
old pair of pantyhose
old rags or scrunched-up pieces of paper
wool or string
EQUIPMENT
scissors

Cut off one of the legs from the pantyhose. Stuff the other leg with the paper or rags right up to the thigh. Tie lengths of wool or string around the toe to make a hairy tip to the tail.

To put on your tail, step into the pants part of the pantyhose and swivel it around until the tail is in the middle of your bottom. If you're wearing a skirt, just let the tail dangle out from beneath it. It looks even better, though, if you undo some of the stitching in the middle back seam of an old pair of jeans to make a hole just big enough to push the tail through.

If there's an old bucket in the laundry with a hole in it, or a used-up detergent bottle, don't throw it out. You'd be amazed at what you can make, or simply do, with this so-called 'junk'!

Leaky Bucket Shower

A leaky bucket still has plenty of uses. Punch an extra couple of holes in the base with a nail or awl and hang it up over a branch in the backyard. Fill it up with water and stand underneath for a cooling shower in the summertime.

Detergent Bottle Water Pistols

Empty detergent bottles, the plastic squeezable kind, can be washed thoroughly and dried, then filled up with water and squeezed as terrific water pistols.

Bottle Raft

This raft will probably only take one or two children. It won't keep you perfectly dry, but it's lots of squishy fun to float on.

INGREDIENTS
dozens of plastic juice bottle with screw-top lids
plastic net bags, such as the ones fruit and vegetables are packed in
string
EQUIPMENT
bodkin or darning needle

Screw all the lids on the bottles. Pack the bottles into the plastic net bags. Depending on the size of the bottles, about 50 bottles will fill about 20 large net bags. Sew up all the bag openings with string and, when you have enough bags, sew them together in a big square.

Snowstorm

INGREDIENTS
**medium-sized jam jar with screw-top lid
enamel paint
small plastic toys, e.g. tiny animals or
little house
waterproof glue
glitter**
EQUIPMENT
paintbrush

Wash and dry the jam jar thoroughly. Paint the lid with the enamel paint and allow it to dry. Glue the plastic toys to the bottom of the jar and set aside to dry. Put about a tablespoon of glitter into the jar. Fill the jar to the top with water and then screw the top on tightly. Shake the jar, then put it down and watch the snow fall.

Jam Jar Tea Set

INGREDIENTS
**6 small squat jars, e.g. jam jars with
snap-off lids rather than screw-on ones
old magazines
coloured paper (optional)
craft glue
lid of a large ice-cream container
clear spray varnish**
EQUIPMENT
**knife
scissors**

Soak the jars to remove the labels, then scrape off any glue left on the jars with the knife. Clean and dry them thoroughly.

Cut out pictures from the old magazines. You can group them together in sets of six if you like, such as flowers or faces, so that each cup will have a different 'personality'. Or just cut out shapes, such as triangles or squares, from coloured paper.

In each set of six picture collections, you need one picture that is big enough to cover the base of the jar. Glue these pictures to the bottom of the jars, face down so that they will show through the jars when they are right way up again. Glue the other pictures around the outside of the jars, overlapping the edges so that no glass may be seen. Set aside to dry the glue.

Decorate the ice-cream container lid in the same way, but gluing the pictures on the inside of the lid, and set aside to dry. When the cups and tray are quite dry, spray them evenly with varnish, allow to dry and spray again.

It's not so long ago that the hard times during the Great Depression prompted parents and children to look at different and novel ways to make inexpensive toys. Often they used scraps of paper or 'rubbish' like cotton reels or milk-bottle caps. Toys like these are just as much fun to make and play with today, even for those of us who have the choice of bigger or more expensive toys.

Tiny Butterfly Top

INGREDIENTS
thin bright blue cardboard
fine black felt-tip pen
bright pink paper
plastic milk-bottle cap
craft glue
plastic toothpick
EQUIPMENT
pencil
scissors
fine skewer
pin

Draw or trace a butterfly shape on the blue cardboard, no more than 4cm (1½in) wide from wing tip to wing tip. Decorate the butterfly shape with your felt-tip pen.

Now draw and cut out a circle from the pink paper that is the same size as the top of the milk-bottle cap. Draw petals and a centre on the pink circle and glue it to the bottle cap top. Use the skewer to punch a hole in the centre of the bottle cap.

Use the pin to make a very tiny hole in the centre of the butterfly. Push the toothpick first through the butterfly, and then through the hole in the bottle cap. The point should be about 6mm (¼in) below the bottom of the cap. Slide the butterfly up the toothpick so that it looks as though it is hovering over the flower. Dot glue around the hole in the cap and the centre of the butterfly so that all fits.

A twist of the fingers will set this little toy twirling.

Milk-bottle Cap Spinning Top

INGREDIENTS
piece of stiff cardboard, 18cm (7in)
square
poster paints
pencil, 16cm (6½in) long
4 milk-bottle caps, washed and dried
thread
EQUIPMENT
compass or saucer
pencil
scissors
paintbrush
needle

Using the compass or the saucer as a guide, pencil a circle on the cardboard and cut it out. Mark the exact centre. Paint a pattern on the card, using your paints. A spiral design will look good, and so will dividing the circle into different pie-shaped segments.

Push the pencil through the centre of the card circle, point-side down. Using the needle, thread the milk-bottle caps onto pieces of thread about 7.5cm (3in) long, and tie them to the top of the pencil. Adjust the threads so that they are all evenly distanced from each other.

When you spin the top, the milk-bottle caps will spin out too.

Cotton Reel Walking Toy

INGREDIENTS
poster paints
wooden cotton reel
rubber band
2 matchsticks
EQUIPMENT
paintbrush

Use the poster paints to decorate the middle of the cotton reel — spots, squiggles or a face will all look good.

Thread the rubber band through the middle of the cotton reel, then put a matchstick through each of the ends of the rubber band. Hold one matchstick steady with one hand and, with the other hand, wind up the toy by twisting the other matchstick around tightly. Place the toy on the table or the floor and it will walk or hop along.

Kitchen Table Hide-out

It's fun to burrow and hide. For a rainy day, nothing beats a cave in the kitchen. To be really secret and feel right, there should be special food to eat in the hide-out, preferably something you don't get to eat all that often, like frankfurts or ice-cream. Oh, and there should a torch too.

EQUIPMENT
old sheets
rug or duvet
books
table and chairs

Spread some sheets over the kitchen table and secure them in the middle with a pile of books. Make a tunnel entrance with a row of chairs and hang a sheet along this too. Take food, toys and rug or duvet inside and hide for ages.

I always think it's nice to have special places to keep other, smaller things in — special boxes, for instance. But don't leave it just at boxes. What about making a zany carry-all from an old shirt?

Shirt Toy Bag

INGREDIENTS
man's old long-sleeved shirt
fabric scraps, rags
fabric paints
strong wooden coathanger
EQUIPMENT
paintbrush

Sew the front and back of the shirt together at the bottom. Sew straight across the ends of the arms. Stuff the arms with the fabric scraps and rags, then sew across the wrists.

Decorate the shirt with the fabric paints — you could paint a tie down the front, or put things climbing up the arms, or draw a scene on it. Hang the shirt on the wooden coathanger and let it dry.

Stitch the hanger to the shirt along the shoulder seams. Hang the toy bag on the back of your bedroom door or in the wardrobe and use it to keep things like toys or Lego in, and to keep your room tidy.

Jeans Carry Bag

Never throw out a pair of old jeans, no matter how tatty they are. They can be used to make a really useful carry bag, with lots of little pockets to carry things like crayons, paper, books, a doll or comb.

Simply cut the legs off the jeans, turn the pants part inside out and stitch in a straight line across the leg openings and across the crotch. If the zipper is still working properly, just zip it up. If not, you may need to stitch the fly closed.

Turn the jeans right side out again. Thread a piece of thick cord or rope through the pants loops. Depending on the size and stiffness of the material, you can use this cord or rope as a drawstring to close the top of the jeans bag. Or stitch or tie two separate lengths of rope or cord to that piece running around the belt loops, and use these as handles or shoulder straps.

Margarine Toy Tubs

*These are very good for keeping all those tiny toys and
pieces of toys in; they stack well, too.*

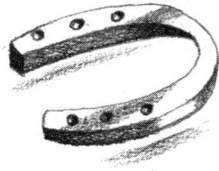

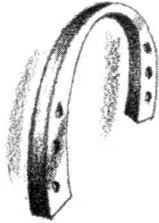

INGREDIENTS
margarine tubs and lids
bright acrylic paints
clear varnish
EQUIPMENT
paintbrush

Wash and dry the margarine tubs and lids. Decorate them
with the bright paints. Allow the tubs to dry, then paint
them with clear varnish.

Horseshoes

This is a great game for the smallest garden or even a
courtyard. It is a game of skill that is fun for people of all ages
and levels of accuracy. It is quite possible for a six-year-old to
get the upper hand over her grandfather!

A horseshoe pitching set should comprise six metal
horseshoes and two stakes, either embedded in a weight or
just driven into the earth. If you live on or near a farm or
horse stud, you will probably be able to get old used shoes for
free. Otherwise you could try hobby shops.

To play, each player stands 1.8m (6ft) back from a stake
and tosses three horseshoes at it, in an attempt to 'collar' the
stake. The winner of the 'best of three', takes an extra 30cm
(1ft) back, while the next player starts at the original 1.8m
(6ft) mark. Whoever wins this round takes another step
back, and so on.

Horseshoes

Chapter Six

IN THE GARDEN

The garden or a park can be a wonderful place to teach children about nature and to encourage them to appreciate its beauty. If you have a crepe myrtle (*Lagerstroemia indica*), for instance, show them how the way the bark changes colour after the rain. Let them roll about in the freshly cut grass or autumn leaves. And show them how to sit quietly and watch the wonderful world of insects and beetles. It doesn't matter if you don't have a garden. Kite flying is best done in a park! And many of the smaller gardening ideas, like the Secret Trail, the Wind Chimes, and the Sun Clock, can be done on a balcony or verandah.

Secret Trail

This is a type of hide-and-seek. Even if you have only a small garden, you can still play.

With a friend, work out some secret signals using sticks and stones. For instance, crossed sticks mean 'not this way', while three set in an arrow shape mean 'straight ahead'. Or you can point to where a secret message is hidden, perhaps under a flower pot. Pebbles can be used to say 'turn right' or 'turn left'.

To play, one person lays the trail and then shows the other where to start and the game is timed. Whoever gets to the end of their trail fastest, wins.

Camouflage

When you're out in the garden, make yourself part of the scenery. Put on your camouflage and climb up in a tree or lie alongside the fence. You can disappear for hours and no one will know where you are ...

INGREDIENTS
green and brown clothes
vines
bunches of leaves
string

Put on green and brown clothes, preferably old ones that you can get dirty without getting into trouble. Make two wreaths from the vines, one to go around your shoulders, and another to frame your face. Make a big fan-like bunch of leaves and tie it together with string. Hold this in front of your face to hide behind.

Picnic

Pack a special picnic lunch to eat in the backyard or a local park. Chicken drumsticks, hard-boiled eggs and carrot sticks are all fun to eat. Carry juice or lemonade in a vacuum flask or screw-top jar — a jug will spill. A treat like an apple and some nuts or raisins is a good idea.

Spread out a rug and put the food on it. Lie back and look at the sky after you've had your lunch. See how many shapes you can find in the clouds. Make a village of little huts from mud and twigs, or smooth flat stones. Make a necklace with daisies or dandelions.

There is something very exciting and romantic about flying a kite — you're connected with the birds and clouds up there by just a piece of string. It's also lots of fun to race around the park or up the beach, wherever you are, trying to keep that kite aloft!

Coloured Paper Kite

INGREDIENTS
coloured paper and/or crepe paper
2 pieces of light dowelling, one 40cm
(16in) long, and one 60cm (24in) long
nails
four small eyelet screws
string
firm paper or plastic
felt-tip pens
poster paints
craft glue
cardboard
long piece of twine
paper or plastic
EQUIPMENT
scissors
hammer
paintbrush

Cut a tail and tassels for the kite from the coloured paper and/or crepe paper.

Place the shorter piece of dowelling over the longer one about a third the way down to form a cross shape. Nail the pieces together. Screw a tiny eyelet screw into each of the four ends of the dowelling. Run a length of string through the four eye holes and tie, forming a diamond shape.

Spread the firm paper or plastic flat on the floor and place the wooden frame on top of it. Trace the outline of the string with a felt-tip pen. Add another 10cm (4in) around all four sides and then cut out the shape. Decorate with paints and felt-tip pens.

Place the wooden frame over the decorated paper or plastic and glue the edges, turning them over the dowelling all the way around. Attach the tail and tassels at each end of the crosswise strip.

Thread a piece of string through each of the eyelet holes. Knot the pieces together in the centre back of the kite; the knot should be about 45cm (18in) out from the frame and exactly at right angles to the intersection of the pieces of dowelling.

Make a spool out of cardboard. Wind the long twine over it. Tie the end of the twine to the knot in the centre of the kite.

Paper Bag Kite

INGREDIENTS
thin cardboard
string
sticky tape
large grocery brown-paper bag
craft glue
poster paints or felt-tip pens
crepe paper
twine or kite string
EQUIPMENT
scissors
paintbrush

Cut out an oval 'ring' of cardboard no larger than the base of the brown-paper bag. Tie three pieces of string, each about 25cm (10in) long, through holes made at equal distances from each other around the

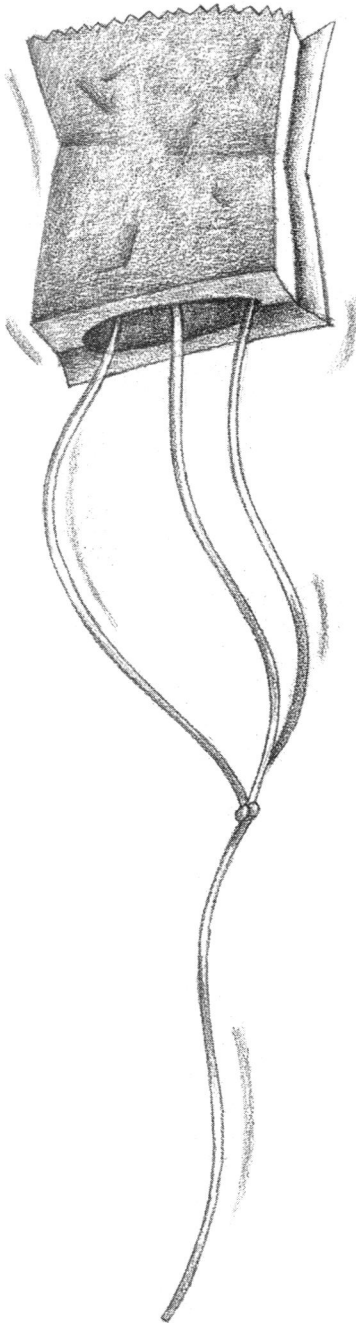

ring. Tape the pieces of string in place for reinforcement.

Trace the inside of the ring onto the flattened bottom of the bag and cut out the hole. Glue the cardboard ring inside the hole to reinforce it. Flip the three strings out.

Decorate the bag with pens or paints and attach crepe-paper streamers to the open end. Tie a long kite string to the knot of the three short strings.

Think about the wonders of the wind. It can be strong enough to rattle windows or even blow roofs off houses, yet gentle enough just to tickle your face and cool you in summertime. The wind is playful — and you can play with it! These projects are all to do with playing with the wind.

Wind Chimes

INGREDIENTS
**thin nylon thread or fine weatherproof string
about 12 different-sized large steel nails
piece of dowelling or narrow plank, approx. 30cm
(12in) long
nails, or 2 eyelet screws and wire or string**

Tie a length of the thread or string to each nail head, then tie the lengths of string along the dowelling or plank at evenly spaced intervals. Hang the nails at different heights, perhaps in a wave pattern, to make it interesting.

Either nail the wind chime to a branch high up in a tree where it will catch the breezes, or make a loop to hang it by, screwing in two eyelet screws to the top of the dowelling or plank and twisting wire or string between them. Hang it high up in the air where the nails will not come near anyone's eyes. Help matters along a little by banging the nails with a stick or spoon, xylophone-style.

Windvane or Weathervane

A windvane is basically a rod, with a vane, or sail, at one end and an arrow at the other. The wind makes the vane turn around, and the arrows indicate from which direction the wind is blowing.

INGREDIENTS

**2 flat pieces of board, 1.5cm (½in) thick and
45cm (18in) long**

nails

stiff cardboard

**piece of dowelling, 2cm (¾in) thick and
45cm (18in) long**

craft glue

string

wooden or plastic cotton reel

steel skewer or steel nail, 10cm (4in) long

EQUIPMENT

pencil

saw

hammer

scissors

drill

I saw you toss a kite on high,

And blow the birds about he sky;

And all around I heard you pass,

Like ladies' skirts across the

grass —

O wind, a-blowing all day long,

O wind, that sings so loud a

song!

ROBERT LOUIS STEVENSON, A CHILD'S
GARDEN OF VERSES (1885)

Saw the corners off the ends of the two flat boards to make into points. Nail them together in the middle to form a cross. Mark the ends of one 'N' and 'S', and the other 'E' and 'W'.

Cut out a semi-circle from the stiff cardboard, about 15cm (6in) long and 10cm (4in) high. This is the vane, or sail. Cut out an arrowhead from the cardboard, 7.5cm (3in) long on each side. Saw two notches at either end of the dowelling — a short one for the arrowhead and a longer one for the vane. Secure the vane and arrowhead in the notches, using glue to make them fit snugly.

Hang the dowelling on a piece of string, sliding the string until you find the point of perfect balance, at or near the

middle. Mark the spot. Drill a hole through the dowelling at this point. The width of the hole should be a bit larger than the skewer so that the pointer will be able to swing around freely on it.

Place a mark in the centre of the crossed boards, place the cotton reel over this mark and then the dowelling on top. Thread the skewer through the hole in the dowelling and the cotton reel, then use a hammer to tap the skewer into the boards until you begin to see the tip of the skewer coming through.

Now position the windvane on top of a fence post or tree stump in a place where there is usually plenty of wind, making sure the 'N' mark faces north. Hammer the skewer down so that it is secure but the pointer swings free.

If you have a vacant sunny spot in your garden, you could use it as the location for a sun clock or a bed of sunflowers.

Sun Clock

INGREDIENTS
large clear plastic lid, approx. 15cm (6in) diameter
felt-tip pen or marking pen
pencil

protractor
skewer
scissors
paper

Use a protractor and a felt-tip or marking pen to mark out 24 equal-spaced radial lines from the centre of the lid. Each of these segments represents one hour of the day, but seeing as the clock can't work at night, you need to mark only those segments that will be hours when there is usually some daylight. Start, for instance, with 5, for 5 am, then go clockwise around the clock face with 6, 7, 8 and so on, up to whatever time it is that it stays light in your area, perhaps 8 pm.

Use the skewer to poke a hole in the exact centre of the clock face, and push the pencil through. The pencil will act both as a stand for the clock and also to cast a shadow on the appropriate hour. Find a bright, sunny spot outside for your sun clock.

Now you need to find out the correct latitude for where you live. (Latitude measures how far you are from the equator.) This information is usually found in an encyclopaedia, or you could ask your local school or library. Make a tracing of the latitude angle and cut out this triangular piece of paper. Point the blunt end of the pencil north if you are in the northern hemisphere, and south if you are in the southern one, and push the pointed end into the ground at an angle to the ground that is close to the latitude triangle. Slide the clock face down the pencil so that it is anchored firmly to the ground. Rotate the clock face until 12 o'clock is directly at the bottom.

For the first couple of readings, you can cheat — run inside and check the time on a watch or clock, then run outside and adjust the sun clock by rotating the face slightly or repositioning the pencil slightly, until the shadow falls on the same number to correspond with the real time. After this, the sun clock should always give you the right time. (You will have to adjust it to take account of daylight saving though!)

Variation: Another idea is to make a simple sundial. Sink a post in a small narrow hole, about 15cm (6in) deep, in the middle of the backyard. Gather together 12 'time markers', such as chunks of timber or clean empty yoghurt tubs. On each one, write a time — 6 am, 7 am, 8 am, right through to 5 pm.

Now, all you need to do is check your watch every hour and run out to push in a time marker where the post's shadow moves to. It's fun to check in a day or two and see the difference in the shadows caused by the daily changes of the movement of the earth around the sun.

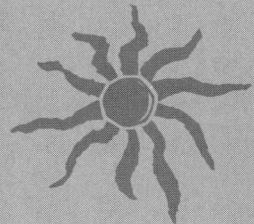

Sun clock

Sunflowers

Sunflowers are lots of fun to grow and they grow fast. Check the seed packet to begin with, as some varieties will grow very tall indeed! The yellow flowers can grow to the size of dinner plates.

Choose a sunny position for your sunflowers. Plant the seed directly into the soil in spring, after any frost is likely to occur. The rows should be 45–60cm (1½–2ft) apart. Cover the seeds lightly with soil, then water them in.

When the seedlings start to appear, support them with stakes, especially if you live in a windy area. (It's a good idea to flag the ends of the stakes with an upended cork or yoghurt carton to stop any accidental injuries to the eyes or face.)

At harvest time, slip netting bags or old stocking feet over the flower heads to collect the dark shiny seeds from the centres of the flowers. You can either dry the seeds in the oven to eat straight away or save them in a paper bag for planting next year.

Birds love to eat the seeds, so if you keep a pet chicken or hen, plant the sunflowers where they can enjoy the seeds when they fall.

Sunlight Experiment

It can be fun experimenting with plants. One project I recall doing when I was growing up had to do with learning about the effect of sunlight on plants. For this project, take a small pot plant, such as a geranium, and cover one leaf with tissue paper, taping it gently into place so as not to bruise the leaf. After a week, take the tissue away and you will see how the leaf has lost its green colour as a result of being deprived of sunlight.

Here is a selection of easy-to-grow activities everyone can enjoy. Even if you don't have a garden, it's a simple matter to grow mustard and cress or make a Root-top Garden on a sunny windowsill.

Mustard and Cress Names

If you're after very quick results, you'll find growing mustard and cress — the fastest crop of all — very satisfying. It's also fun if you do not have access to a garden, as mustard and cress will grow on newspaper, cloth or absorbent paper.

Take a shallow foil or plastic tray and cover the base with cottonwool, towelling or absorbent paper. Wet this thoroughly. Sow the seed thickly in the shape of the letters of your name, then put the tray in a shady place for a day or two.

When the seeds have sprouted, put the tray in full light and keep it damp. When the little plants are about 7.5cm (3in) high, they may be snipped off with scissors and used whole or chopped in salads or sandwiches. Sow seed every 10–14 days for a continuous supply.

Variation: Try Virginian stock (*Malcolmia maritima*) seed instead of mustard and cress. Sow the initials or letters of your name densely with the seeds, then water in well.

Sprouting Seeds

Sprouts grow easily just about anywhere and they are fun to eat.

INGREDIENTS
wide-mouthed glass jar
seeds, e.g. alfalfa, mung bean, radish
piece of fine netting or pantyhose
rubber band

Rinse out the jar thoroughly. Put the seeds in the bottom of the jar and cover them with water. Cap the jar with the piece of fine netting or cut out a square of pantyhose and secure to the top with the rubber band. Leave for 10 minutes, then up end the jar to strain out the water.

Shake the jar so that the seeds are evenly distributed along the inside, not clumped together. Then lay the jar on its side in a warm, light place (but not in direct sunlight). Repeat the watering and shaking process each day until the seeds sprout.

Variation: Beans and peas also germinate quickly and so are excellent sprouting subjects for indoor fun and simple nature experiments.

Take a round, wide-necked jar and run a thick fold of blotting paper around the inside. Slot a few beans or peas between the paper and the glass and the pour some water in the bottom of the jar so that the blotting paper sucks it up to the beans and peas.

Within a few days they will germinate, the shoots growing up and the leaves developing, while through the glass you will be able to see the roots growing downwards for anchorage.

Growing Garlic

Garlic is easy to plant and grow. Plant a few cloves, pointy end uppermost, about 2.5cm (1in) deep in potting mix in a small pot (not too close). Water the cloves gently and check every couple of days to make sure the soil is slightly damp but not wet, as garlic does not like wet feet. After a couple of weeks, long narrow leaves will pop up, which may be snipped and used on sandwiches and in salads.

Taking Cuttings

It's easy to take cuttings from certain plants and flowers, such as easy-to-grow geraniums, coleus and busy lizzies (Impatiens spp.).

First, remove the lower leaves from the stem, leaving at least two pairs of leaves on top. It's best to nip off any flowers, as these may drain energy the cutting needs to produce roots and become a new plant.

Dip the cut end of the cutting in starter mix (available from plant nurseries), then plant the cutting about 2.5–5cm (1–2in) deep, depending on the length of the cutting itself, into a punnet box or box filled with good-quality potting mix. Drip water in gently to moisten the potting mix thoroughly, then water gently or mist every other day, or as needed.

Set aside a shelf, windowsill or low table in a sunny position where you can look after your collection of cuttings in various stages of growth.

Growing Bulbs

You don't always need soil to grow flowers. Over many centuries, bulbs have been grown in just water, and taken inside to decorate rooms. Hyacinth and narcissus bulbs are both suitable for this experiment.

Sit the bulb on top of a bottle or small jam jar so that it fits snugly, with its roots hanging down into the water. (An empty yoghurt tub is usually a good choice too.) You must make sure that the water level is kept up to the roots as they develop, but that only the very base of the bulb ever touches the water. You should also add a small chip of charcoal to the water to stop it from souring.

Put the bulb jar in a darkish place until the roots are about 7.5–10cm (3–4in) long, then bring it out into the light. Continue to keep the water level up to the roots, and the bulb should throw up a stem and a flower if kept in a warm sunny spot.

I wandered lonely as a cloud

That floats on high o'er vales and hills,

When all at once I saw a crowd,

A host, of golden daffodils;

Beside the lake, beneath the trees,

Fluttering and dancing in the breeze.

WILLIAM WORDSWORTH, 'I WANDERED LONELY AS A CLOUD' (1815)

Root-top Gardens

It is interesting and fun to grow a 'garden' from the tops of root vegetables.

Cut the top off a carrot, turnip or parsnip, leaving 6mm (¼in) of the root and 6mm (¼in) of the leaf stem.

Put a layer of pebbles or stones on the bottom of a shallow bowl or saucer of water. Stand the root tops, leaf stumps uppermost, on top of the pebbles and leave the container on a sunny windowsill. Quite soon, the root tops will sprout new leaves and roots.

If you have eaten a fresh pineapple, save the top, as this will also sprout quickly.

Pip Pots

Every time you have a piece of fruit, save the pip or stone. Many of these will germinate successfully to form attractive plants. Oranges, lemons, dates, tomatoes and even more exotic fruits such as mangoes, lychees and avocados will soon shoot if they are planted in a peat-based compost. It's a good idea to soak hard pips, like avocado stones, for a couple of days before planting.

INGREDIENTS
4 small plant pots with saucers
potting mix
4 types of pips or stones
4 clean glass jars (with a
circumference approx. the same
as the top of the pot)

Fill the pots with the potting mix and push two pips or stones into the top of the mixture, then cover. Label each pot with the name of the fruit you are hoping to grow — for example, date, plum, cherry, orange, lemon or apricot. Dampen each pot but do not saturate with water.

Upturn a glass jar over the middle of each pot, creating a miniature glasshouse. Keeping a constant temperature and state of humidity will encourage the pip or stone to sprout. Place the pots in a warm place away from direct sunlight.

The pips or stones could take up to a month to sprout, so check every few days to see that the potting mix is still moist — not wet — and dampen with a fine mist if necessary. When the pip or stone has sprouted, take off the glass jar and put the pot outside or on a porch where there is plenty of light and air.

Even if you don't want actually to set to and grow a plant, you will find that plants and flowers are endlessly interesting.

Looking at Plants

There are some really tiny plants — mosses, of course, or you could ask at a nursery about plants called saxifrage and oregano and the Sempervium species — that are really small and intricate to look at.

Cacti are tough and hardy, and fascinating to grow. Christmas cactus (*Zygocactus spp.*) with its flat segmented stems and garish pink and red flowers will lend a zany air to a windowsill. The rather revolting rat's-tail cactus (*Aporocactus flagelliformis*), with its long, hairy, ratty-looking stems, is much admired by small boys. The South American pebble plant (*Lithops spp.*) is another appealing little oddity, which will suit a sunny spot in a bedroom. One variety worth finding is *Lithops optica*, the window plant, which is almost entirely buried in the soil apart from one translucent little 'window' on the surface that allows light to reach the rest of the plant. Truth is surely stranger than fiction when it comes to the world of plants.

Note for the grown-ups: Cacti need to be kept out of the reach of younger children.

Plants That Do Things

There are also lots of things you can do with plants, rather than just look at them. For instance, fuschia buds are very satisfying to pop, and the Australian Grevillea longifolia makes a great 'toothbrush'. (Be sure to ask first, though — adults may not like you doing some of these things to their prize flowerbed!)

The poached-egg plant (*Limnanthes douglasii*) has lovely open-faced yellow and white flowers, which can be most obligingly used for pretend egg dishes.

And what garden, no matter how small, would be complete without snapdragons (*Antirrhinum spp.*)? These plants produce masses of wonderfully shaped flowers, which can be worn as caps on the end of one's nose. Snapdragons also make terrific finger puppets.

Time-of-day plants are interesting too. For instance, the blue flowers of morning glory (*Ipomoea spp.*) start to come open with the first rays of sunshine but will be closed by midday. Dandelions (*Crepis spp.*), of course, are well loved for their ability to tell the time.

And then there's the funny sensitive plant (*Mimosa pudica*). Running your fingers gently over the leaves will cause them quickly to close together in pairs.

Selecting Plants

Perhaps you will be able to go the local nursery to select some plants of your own. Some that might interest you are:

- **lamb's ears** (*Stachys lanata*) because they are soft and velvety, just like a lamb's ears, in fact;
- **moses-in-a-basket** (*Rhoeo spathacea*), with its tiny little 'baby' flower nestled in the leaves;
- **angel's fishing rod** (*Dierama pulcherrimum*), for its intriguing name as much as for its very pretty bell-shaped flowers;
- **foxgloves** (*Digitalis spp.*), for dolls' hats — beware, though, this is a poisonous plant;
- **shrimp bush** (*Beloperone guttata*), with its pink flowers that really do look exactly like prawns; or
- **goldfish plant** (*Nematanthus wettsteinii*), with its fat yellow flowers that 'swim' in a nest of leaves.

Plant Collections

If you are interested in a particular group of plants — alpines, for instance, or begonias, or odd-shaped cacti — you might like to subscribe to the appropriate specialist society. Ask the grown-ups what they think.

Note for the grown-ups: A very old and lovely idea is to plant a tree for each child in a family. Make a note of the tree's birthday and each year take a photo of the child next to their tree.

There are lots of things living in a garden or park other than just plants or trees. Bugs, caterpillars, butterflies, worms, lizards, even ants, all play a vital role in the web of life and in maintaining a healthy ecosystem. A great way to learn about the complexities of plant and animal life is to study a caterpillar turning into first a chrysalis and then a beautiful butterfly or moth.

Butterfly Farm

INGREDIENTS
shoe box
fine netting (shadecloth is ideal)
thread
small branches or sprigs of a suitable plant (the one on which you find the caterpillar)
small garden pot full of slightly damp soil or potting mix
caterpillar
big rubber band
EQUIPMENT
scissors
needle or stapler

Cut out one of the long sides of the shoe box and cut the netting to cover. Stitch or staple into place.

Push the branches or sprigs into the pot. Place the pot and food plant into the box and gently put the caterpillar onto the leaves. Remember that caterpillars have no bones and are easily squished — try to roll the caterpillar into the box and onto the leaves, rather than pick it up between thumb and fingers.

Put the lid back on the shoe box, securing with the rubber band if it is likely to be tipped up by other children.

Replace the plant material with fresh branches every day and clean up any caterpillar droppings. The caterpillar should soon turn into a chrysalis and, after that, the butterfly or moth will emerge. You should not touch the new insect until its wings are quite dry.

When it is starting to flutter about the box, take the box back out to the plant on which the caterpillar was found, take the lid off gently and let the butterfly or moth leave when it is ready. If it doesn't immediately fly away, gently ease your finger under its feet and pop it onto a leaf so that it can safely prepare itself for flight.

Worm Farm

INGREDIENTS
large container (the foam cartons used to pack fresh fruit and vegetables in are ideal)
bedding material, e.g. peat moss, shredded paper, leaf mould and straw or grass clippings mixture, or a combination of all three
soil
compost
food, e.g. kitchen scraps
earthworms
shadecloth, hessian or weed-control matting

Half-fill the container with the bedding material. Moisten the bedding material until it is just possible to squeeze a few drops of water from it. To this layer, add a thin layer (5cm/2in) of soil, then another slightly thicker layer (10cm/4in) of compost and then sprinkle a bit more soil on top.

A good position for the box is the back verandah where it is protected from direct sun and, preferably, rain. Direct sun can make the box too hot for the worms, while the rain can make it too wet, possibly fouling the soil and killing the worms. If the box has to go outside, drainage holes must be provided.

Introduce the worms to the box once the compost has cooled. You can start with one or two pairs — it won't take long before there are a lot more! Before popping them into the box, bury some food for them just beneath the surface, scratching the soil over it to cover lightly. Almost any dead organic matter can be used — kitchen scraps, poultry pellets, seaweed, manure and leaves are all suitable. Large pieces, such as cabbage leaves and chunks of cauliflower, should be chopped up first.

Put the worms on top of the soil over the buried food and they will soon wriggle downwards to escape the light.

Cover the box loosely with the shadecloth, hessian or weed-control matting to exclude light and reduce moisture loss.

The amount you feed your earthworms can be worked out by trial and error. Simply, the more worms there are, the greater their ability to dispose of uneaten kitchen scraps, manure and so on. If you find that scraps are remaining uneaten near the surface, reduce the amount until the number of worms increases.

Other worm-farming management tips to remember are to check the aeration of the soil by gently poking the surface with a fork every couple of weeks, and to sprinkle the soil with water every 2–7 days, depending on the time of year, to maintain the correct moisture content, based on the 'squeeze test'.

Finally, if you want to turn your hobby to profit, try selling the worms to the local fishing club, organic gardeners or nurseries. If you want nice fat worms to sell, add poultry pellets or meal to their food.

Bird Feeder Ball

Suet, or fat, is attractive to birds who are insectivores (eat insects) and require fatty foods to keep their body energy high.

INGREDIENTS
breadcrumbs, birdseed and melted suet or suet and dripping
cord
large button
EQUIPMENT
small plastic bowl

Mix up a handful each of the breadcrumbs, birdseed and melted suet or suet and dripping in the bowl. Thread a long piece of the cord with the button, knot to secure, and mould the mixture around it to form a ball, leaving the button on the bottom. Leave the mixture in the bowl to set so that the cord forms a 'wick' through the centre of the ball, which is held in place by the button plug.

When it is firm, tie the bird feeder ball to a tree. Put it out only in very cold weather, as it tends to rot quickly.

Variation: Another way to make a bird feeder is to use a coconut. First, use a saw to cut off the top of the coconut, then remove the milk. Using an awl, make a hole in the base. Thread a piece of thick string, approximately 60cm (2ft) long, through the hole and tie a large knot to stop it from running through. Fill the coconut half with the same suet-and-seed mixture as above and press down firmly. Leave the mixture to set. Hang the filled shell outside your house, high up in a tree.

Turnip Traps

There are plenty of good and friendly creatures that are worth encouraging to your garden, like frogs (which eat mosquitoes), worms (which turn the soil over) and bees (which pollinate the flowers). However, some really are pests, like slugs and snails, and they will eat all the new shoots and seedlings you are trying to grow.

Rather than use sprays or powders to get rid of garden pests, which can be dangerous to children as well as pets, try making turnip traps.

Cut several large turnips in half and hollow out the insides. Carve out a tiny curved door in the side of each turnip half. Place the turnip halves, cut-side down, around the garden. Snails and slugs will be attracted to the moist underside of the turnip house and will creep inside through the doorway. Next day you will be able to

Bird Feeder Ball

dispose of them. Orange or grapefruit halves and hollowed-out apples also work well.

Beer Trap

Slugs and snails are famous tipplers — they like alcohol so much that they will drown in it!

INGREDIENTS
empty jam jar
little stale beer or dark ale

Dig a little hole in a garden bed where snails and slugs have been eating the plants. The hole should be deep enough to hold the jar so that the lid of the jar is level with the soil. Place a couple of centimetres (1in) of stale beer or ale at the bottom of the jar. Next day you will find several dead slugs and snails there.

When I was little my mother would do this and she would tell me that at least they died happy.

You may not have your own garden, but that doesn't mean that you can't make something similar. What about an aquarium so that you can study a pet fish? Or a miniature garden that you can play with on a balcony or in a courtyard?

Water Garden

You can make a very simple water garden from a shallow aluminium foil tray or an old plastic ice-cream tub. Sink the container into the ground and plant around the rim with creeping ground covers and tiny bulbs, like narcissi.

Aquarium

INGREDIENTS
large glass jar
gravel or pebbles
goldfish and greenery (from pet shops)
fish food

Wash and dry the jar and rinse the gravel or pebbles thoroughly under the tap to get rid of any residue that might taint the water. Put the gravel in the bottom of the jar and plant the greenery.

Carefully pour in room-temperature water — don't just use cold water straight from the tap. Run the water into the sink first, add a dash of hot water, then let it stand for an hour before using a cup or jug to scoop it into the jar. This way, some of the chlorine that is present in tap water will evaporate too.

Pop the fish in, and feed it with fish food. Change some of the water regularly. If you get more than one fish, it's a good idea to invest in a fish tank as the extra fish will need more space and more oxygen from plants.

Rainbow Garden

How about a rainbow garden? Nearly 100 years ago a famous English gardening writer, Gertrude Jekyll, proposed this pretty idea.

Mark out six or seven curved strips in a flowerbed, and plant every strip in different-coloured flowers to match the colours of the rainbow. So you might have strips of red hot pokers, yellow marigolds, purple pansies, blue forget-me-nots, pink alyssum and so on.

Annuals such as hot pink portulaca and blue lobelia will survive an amateur scatter-planting and grow practically anywhere. Orange or yellow nasturtiums have nice fat seeds and quickly germinate to form a colourful display.

Variation: Mix up annual seeds — pink petunias, phlox, red nasturtiums and blue cornflowers, for instance — and scatter the mixture over a bald corner of the garden, resulting in an exciting and never-before-seen colour combination.

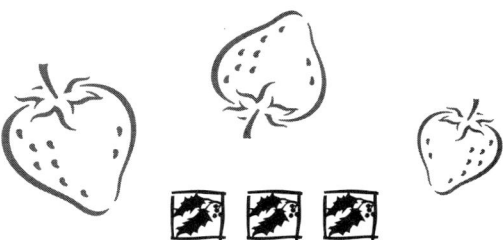

Spring Strawberry Pot

INGREDIENTS
piece of rubber hose, the same length as the depth of the pot
purchased terracotta strawberry pot
potting mix or loam
shorter pieces of hose (each approx. 15cm/6in long), one for each pot pocket
punnet of strawberry runners (perpetual varieties are best)
EQUIPMENT
metal skewer

This is a project for early spring. Pierce the piece of rubber hose with the skewer every few centimetres or so, and place it upright in the centre of the strawberry pot. Pour in the potting mix or loam around the hose and pack down lightly, filling up to the rim.

Pierce the shorter lengths of hose and push into the pot's pockets. Spoon extra mix into the pockets, firming it lightly around the lengths of hose.

Break up the strawberry plantlets, being careful not to damage any runners, and tuck one or two into each pot pocket. Plant the rest in the top of the pot. Water the whole pot thoroughly to bed the plantlets in.

Check the soil every day or so, as these pots tend to dry out quickly and strawberries prefer a slightly damp soil. When it is getting dry, water by pouring water into the hose ends. This way the roots will get a good drink and you will not run the risk of wetting any fruit, and so causing it to rot. Keep the pot away from cold or frost.

The flowers and eventually the fruit will trail attractively over the sides of the terracotta pot.

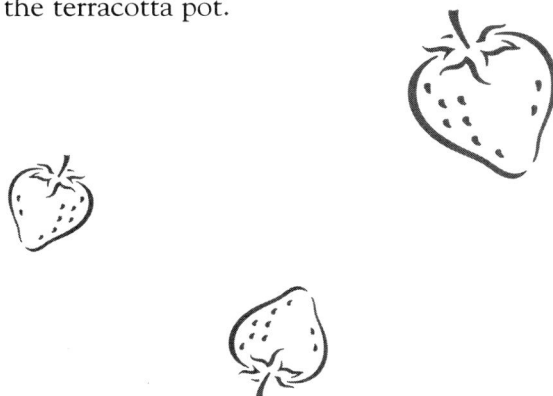

Thumbelina Pots

INGREDIENTS
clay (from craft shops)
tempera paints
clear varnish
soil
moss
EQUIPMENT
sheet of paper
little paintbrush

Roll a piece of clay into a small ball. Press it against the table to form a base. Push your thumb into the top of the ball, then work around it, pressing the clay into a pot shape with the thumb and forefinger. Put the pot on a sheet of paper to dry. Repeat with other pieces of clay until you have a collection of pots.

When the pots are quite dry, decorate them with dots, dashes or squiggles, then apply a coat of clear varnish. Fill them with a little soil and grow moss in them.

Rock Garden

Collect together some leftover pieces of landscaping rock or stones, pack them together with soil and plant the cracks with small succulents, herbs, bulbs and tufty grasses. Keep the watering up in the rock garden, as it will dry out quickly, especially in summer.

Miniature Garden

This is a good project if you have only a small garden, or even no garden at all.

INGREDIENTS
suitable container, e.g. old ice-cream container, old baking tray, shallow terracotta tray or waterproofed wooden box
gravel
potting mix and compost
foil or small mirror
extra plant pots or saucers
pebbles and stones
small plants or seeds (small geraniums, lobelias, alyssum, stock, Johnny jump-up violets and dwarf French marigolds are all good)

Half-fill the container with gravel, then top up with the potting mix and compost (leaf mould is best).

Lay the piece of foil or the mirror on the soil (this is the lake). You can bury the extra plant pots or saucers, upended, in the soil as you go to create mountains and hills as a backdrop to the garden. Make roads, walls and bridges from the pebbles and stones. Hobby shops have a great choice of little figurines, animals and Japanese-style temples that you might be able to buy too.

Fill in the spaces with plants or cuttings. For a very small garden, an ordinary tablespoon is a better planting tool than a regular trowel. Use any of the small plants mentioned above, or dig up small plants mentioned above, or dig up small mosses or clumps of fern and grass from the garden and plant them.

Map Garden

What about a map garden? This is a particularly good idea if you are learning about your country at school. Trace out a map of the country in a flowerbed where the soil is soft, then dig out tiny ditches for rivers, plant little bushes or herbs for trees, and use stones to make cities and skyscrapers.

Bottle Garden

Any small ornamental plants usually grown indoors are suitable for bottle gardens. They need to be reasonably slow growing so that they do not swamp the bottle. Ivy (Hedera spp.) is good, as are African violets (Saintpaulia spp.), small ferns such as maidenhair ferns, mosses, begonias or creeping fig (Ficus pumila). A desert-style bottle garden, containing only tiny cacti or similar succulent plants, is easiest of all. Use sand, gravel and pebbles — even a colourful china Mexican figurine! — and all you need do is mist the garden occasionally.

INGREDIENTS

reasonably flat-based glass bottle with wide mouth, e.g. wine flagon, large biscuit jar, lolly jar
small stones or gravel
sand
light, dry, sandy soil
charcoal (optional)
tiny plants and seedlings
bark and twigs
cork or cap

EQUIPMENT

paper funnel
small sponge
long, thin bamboo canes or wooden skewers
masking tape
baby's spoon and fork
tweezers
fine tube or mister

Wash and dry the bottle thoroughly, and lay it on its side.

Line the bottom of the bottle garden with small stones or gravel, then sprinkle with sand. Using the paper funnel so as not to make a mess around the bottle sides, pour in a few centimetres of the sandy soil. Mix the soil with a little charcoal if you like, as this will stop the soil from souring. Clean the sides of the bottle as you go, using a small sponge attached to a bamboo cane or wooden skewer.

Collect together a selection of tiny plants and seedlings (the smaller the better, making them easier to introduce through the bottle's neck). Tape the baby's spoon and the fork to the bamboo canes or wooden skewers, and use these to plant the seedlings where you want. Then tape the tweezers handles to bamboo canes or skewers to create extra-long handles. Use the tweezers to move the plants about, placing the tall ones in the centre or at the back. Bark, twigs and tiny rocks can be used to secure the plants in place.

Once planting is completed, water using a fine tube or mister, or trickle water carefully down the sides of the bottle. Do not overwater as this will cause the plants to stagnate. Cork or cap the bottle. You will easily be able to tell whether there is too much or too little water in your bottle garden by the third day, when there should be condensation on the inside of the top. If there isn't, mist in a little extra water and reseal. If it's really drippy, leave the cap off for a day or so to allow your mini-environment to rebalance itself.

Keep the bottle garden in a light-filled room, but away from direct sunlight, and turn it around regularly.

Bottle Garden

There are so many things to do in a garden, even a small one. Are there any damp corners where snails might be lurking? You can collect them and have a snail race! And if you've got an old piece of heavy plastic or tarpaulin lying about, how about making a water whoosher on a hot day?

Water Whoosher

Has your backyard got a bit of a slope? Good! It will be easy for you to make this water slide when there are no water restrictions.

INGREDIENTS
**large plastic sheet or drop cloth (from boating supplies shop or discount chain store)
2 or 3 large rocks or bricks**

Arrange the plastic sheet or drop cloth over a curving area of grass (not a hard surface) and secure at the higher side with the rocks or bricks.

Position the sprinkler at the top end of the sheet and turn it on so that the spray falls on the plastic sheeting until it is quite wet.

Now, start your slides and rolls. If you get a good run-up, you can slide the whole length of the sheet on your stomach!

Bug Races

INGREDIENTS
piece of cardboard, 45cm (18in) square
felt-tip pen

Place the piece of cardboard flat on the ground. Use the felt-tip pen to mark a starting point in the middle.

Collect together some garden bugs, such as ants, ladybirds, caterpillars, beetles, worms or snails. (Leave spiders and centipedes alone!) Put them gently in the middle of the cardboard at the start point and sit down to watch and see how quickly they get to the edge. Don't prod them, and let them go back to the garden when you've finished.

Variation: Another idea is to have a snail race. For this you need a piece of glass and a snail for each person playing. The fun part is to watch the snails oozing along from underneath the glass. You can see how they slide along.

Nature Diary

With so many wonderful nature crafts and toys to make and projects to experiment with, you should record your work in a diary. This soon becomes something of a calendar of the seasons, you will find, and it will be really exciting to compare last year's progress with the present, and so on.

Bug Catcher

You can buy these, but it's a good idea to know how to make one quickly if you want to have a close look at something you've just found.

INGREDIENTS
piece of fine netting or plastic cling wrap
empty glass jar
rubber band
EQUIPMENT
scissors
skewer

Cut a circular piece out of the netting large enough to go over the top of the jar and a little bit down the sides. Secure it with the rubber band. Alternatively, tear off a piece of plastic cling wrap and put this over the top of the jar, then pop some holes in it with a skewer so that the bug you have caught can breathe.

Now, go on safari round the garden. Look carefully among the leaf litter for wildlife, such as caterpillars, ants and millipedes. It's a good idea to wear gardening gloves for this game, just to be on the safe side.

Wishing Games

Moon penny bright as silver

Come and play with little

children.

Whenever there was a small, skinny little new moon in the sky, my mother would always say, 'New moon, turn your money over'. A new moon is said to be very lucky, and means a new start or a new chance. To make a wish on a new moon, you should turn your back to it, and then look at it over your left shoulder. Another special moon wish/prayer/lucky charm is:

I see the moon and the moon sees me
God bless the moon, and God bless me.

Or you can say to the first star in the evening sky:

Star light, star bright,
First star I see tonight,
Wish I may, wish I might
have the wish I wish tonight.

Chapter Seven

LOTS OF OTHER THINGS TO MAKE AND DO

Hey diddle, diddle, the cat and the fiddle

The cow jumped over the moon;

The little dog laughed to see such sport

And the dish ran away with the spoon.

This book is really only meant to be a starting point. Once you start looking around at all the wonderful things you can make and do with found materials, you are only limited by your imagination.

Wall of Stars

It's exciting to learn about the stars and the planets. Cut out lots of shiny star shapes from foil or, better still, glow-in-the-dark paper (from the newsagents) and stick them on the wall. Look up a book about astronomy and see if you can copy some of the constellations and patterns you see in the sky at night. Add some shooting stars and a space ship too.

Note for the grown-ups: Any project involving dye or paint can get pretty messy, so adult supervision is advised. Always put down plenty of old newspapers on the floor or table work surface first, to avoid any problems later!

Tie-dyeing

INGREDIENTS
cold-water fabric dye
white fabric or T-shirt
EQUIPMENT
old plastic bucket
rubber bands
rubber gloves
stick or old wooden spoon
scissors

Make up the dye in the bucket, according to the manufacturer's instructions.

Roll up or pleat the fabric or T-shirt.

Slip the rubber bands tightly around the fabric at intervals (this will create a wiggly white stripe, because the dye will not be able to reach it).

Put on your rubber gloves. Place the fabric or T-shirt in the bucket of dye, stirring gently with a stick or old wooden spoon. Still with the rubber gloves on, lift the fabric into the sink and rinse, according to the manufacturer's instructions (usually one rinse in hot water, then a second in cold).

Leave the wet fabric or T-shirt on a pile of old newspapers to dry. When it is dry, cut away the rubber bands.

Onion Skin Dyed T-shirt

INGREDIENTS
4 brown onions
white T-shirt
EQUIPMENT
old stocking or pantyhose foot
large saucepan
rubber bands
straight stick or long-handled
wooden spoon
scissors

Peel off the brown outer skins of the onions, place them in the stocking foot and tie in a knot to secure. Place the onion skins in a large saucepan of boiling water and cook for 20 minutes.

Meanwhile, make tie-markings in the T-shirt by first rolling or pleating it up, and

Natural Dyes

Plenty of other natural things will yield a dye for clothing (or eggs too). Try using different varieties of yellow or reddish-coloured gum leaves, or pieces of bark. Geranium petals and red or purple dahlia heads also make terrific dyes.

then slipping rubber bands tightly around the fabric at intervals so that the dye will not be able to reach these sections. Put the T-shirt in the saucepan and reduce the heat, simmering for 1 hour. Make sure the T-shirt stays submerged by pushing under the water with the wooden spoon or the stick.

Remove the saucepan from the heat, strain off the T-shirt and allow it to cool. Rinse it gently and quickly in cold water, then leave on a pile of old newspapers or towels to dry. When it is dry, cut away the rubber bands to reveal the pattern.

Making Crystals

INGREDIENTS
warm water
salt
vinegar
porous stones, such as pumice or coal
EQUIPMENT
shallow bowl
tablespoon

Fill the bowl with the warm water. Start adding salt to the water, a spoonful at a time, stirring after each addition until the salt dissolves. Keep doing this until no more salt will dissolve. Now add two tablespoons of vinegar to the mixture and stir that in.

Pile the porous stones into the bowl so that they stick out the top like mountains. In less than a day, salt crystals will start to 'grow' on top of the stones in long and interesting tree-like shapes.

Bread Dough Pendants

INGREDIENTS
1 cup plain flour, sifted
½ cup salt
warm water, to mix
several pieces of thin macaroni
gloss enamel paints
clear varnish
ribbon or leather thonging
EQUIPMENT
medium-sized bowl
rolling pin
bread board
small cookie cutters, e.g. heart, star
egg slice
baking sheet
paintbrush

Preheat the oven to 100°C (212°F). Combine the flour and salt in the bowl and add enough warm water to form a firm dough. Knead the dough until it is soft, then roll it out on the bread board to approximately 1.5cm (½in) thick. Use the cookie cutters to cut out shapes for pendants.

Pick them up with an egg slice and put them on a baking sheet. Press the pieces of macaroni at the top of the shapes to form holes to hang the pendants by later. Bake the dough in the oven until it is quite hard. Test by pressing with a finger — if the dough gives, it is not ready — but be careful not to burn the shapes either.

Remove the dough shapes from the oven and allow to cool completely before decorating with bright enamel paint. When the paint is dry, paint the pendants with varnish, and thread them on a ribbon or leather thong.

Secret Messages

Candle ends are very useful things, even in these days of electric light. Write secret messages with a candle end on paper. The only way anyone will know what you have said is if they paint over the wax message, which will make the words show up.

Variation: How about making up a code? One idea is to first spell each word backwards, and then add a letter to each word. Another is to write all the letters of the message together as one long word, then divide the long word into three different strips of paper and send these.

Coming up are lots of puppet ideas. Why not make several puppets and give each one a personality? You could even put on a puppet show for your family.

Felt Finger Puppet Family

INGREDIENTS
coloured felt
thread
small scraps of coloured felt, tiny buttons or beads, wool, silk, pipe-cleaners, cottonwool, foil
craft glue
EQUIPMENT
scissors
needle
4 wooden clothes pegs
glass or cup

Cut out 4 pieces of felt, each approximately 4 x 6cm (1½ x 2½in). Fold them in half lengthwise and oversew the long sides. Turn them inside out.

Clip the clothes pegs around the side of a glass or cup and sit the felt tubes over the pegs.

Now decorate them by gluing on the small scraps of coloured felt, buttons, beads and so on, to make faces, hair and tiny outfits of your choice. Seeing as it is a family, you could give them all matching hair or little pipe-cleaner spectacles.

Leave the puppets to dry on the clothes pegs before you play with them.

Eskimo Finger Masks

The Inuit Eskimos of northern Canada, Alaska and Greenland have been using these tiny little masks in their traditional plays for many centuries.

INGREDIENTS
clay
tempera paints
EQUIPMENT
cookie cutters
toothpick or skewer
tiny paintbrush

Take a small piece of clay and flatten it till it is about as thick as your finger. Use a cookie cutter to cut out a circle, star or diamond.

Take two more pieces of clay and roll two thin snake-like coils; each should be long enough to go around the flat shape. Moisten the edges of the shape and the coils, and press the coils around the outside of the shape.

Make two more smaller coils, about twice as long and as thick as your finger. Join the ends so that you have two circles large enough to fit around your first and middle fingers. Moisten the edges of these finger loops where they will join the edges of the shape and press them together. Make a few more very thin coils and gently press and smooth these all around the join to strengthen it.

Mark out a face or pattern on the shape with the toothpick or skewers. Paint or decorate. Make hair with lots of tiny little coils of clay and press onto the shape while it is still damp.

Here's the lady's knives and

forks

Here's the lady's table

Here's the lady's looking-glass

And here's the baby's cradle.

Rubber Glove Octopus

I didn't have a use for old rubber gloves that had holes in the fingertips until my son Edward invented this five-tentacled octopus one day.

EQUIPMENT
old rubber glove
felt-tip pens

Put on the rubber glove. Use the felt-tip pens to draw an octopus face in the middle of the palm with a great big black eye. Draw suckers on the textured undersides of the fingers and thumb.

Egg Carton Frog

INGREDIENTS
cardboard egg carton
green paint
black pipe-cleaner
craft glue
scraps of black, red and white felt
EQUIPMENT
scissors
paintbrush
stapler

Open out the egg carton and cut the bottom in half. Do not cut the top of the lid. Close the carton and paint it all green with black spots except for the two

ends — paint a top and bottom red mouth on these. Close the lid, fitting the tabs in place.

Glue or staple a black pipe-cleaner tongue to the centre of the lid, curling the end slightly. Fold the egg carton in half forward so that the tongue pops out from between the red lips. Make eyes from the felt and glue in place.

Make the frog puppet 'talk' by opening and shutting the front of the carton.

Papier-mâché Puppets

INGREDIENTS
wallpaper paste
thin cardboard
craft glue
1 newspaper, torn into long thin strips
poster paints
decorating materials, e.g. wool, rope, foil,
crepe paper, feathers, string, beads,
buttons, lace, fringing
fabric remnants
thread

2 plastic buckets
scissors
stapler
newspapers
wooden spoon
bottle or jar
thin pieces of dowelling, or long sticks
flat bristle paintbrushes
needle

Mix the wallpaper paste up in one bucket, according to the manufacturer's instructions. Let it stand for 15 minutes while you make up the puppets' necks.

For the necks, cut six strips of thin cardboard, each about 5 x 10cm (2 x 4in). Roll them around your finger to form a tube and staple or glue shut.

Cover the working surface with newspaper. Put the newspaper strips into the second bucket and pour in the wallpaper paste, stirring with your hands or the wooden spoon. Pick up three or four of the gluey strips and start to roll them into a small ball. Set the ball onto the top of one of the cardboard necks and secure it by winding more gluey strips around and about it. Build up the puppet's head, shaping more strips into a nose, eyebrows, horns, goggle eyes, big ears and so on. Repeat with the other heads. Sit the necks over the sticks or the dowelling and leave them in bottles or jars to dry.

When they are quite dry, the puppet heads can be painted then decorated with wool or rope hair, feathers and beads. Make crowns or hats out of the foil and crepe paper.

To finish, cut out the puppets' clothes from the fabric remnants. For each puppet, you will need a piece approximately 30 x 75cm (12 x 30in). Gather the short edge to fit around the base of the puppet's neck and glue in place. Sew up the back of the fabric.

You should be able to make the puppets move by waggling your fingers.

Paper Bag Owl

INGREDIENTS
scrap paper
sticky tape
toilet roll tube
brown-paper bag
wool
coloured paper
craft glue
EQUIPMENT
scissors

Squash a sheet of scrap paper into a ball and sticky tape it into the top of the toilet roll tube. Place it inside the paper bag and tie a piece of wool under the ball, forming a head and neck. Cut out ears, big eyes and a beak from the coloured paper and stick them in place.

You should be able to make the puppet move by sticking your hand inside the bag and one or two fingers up the toilet roll tube.

Hand Shadows

Experiment with the different shapes and movements your hands can make. You can make a bird with flapping wings, a dog with a tail, or a mouth that opens and shuts.

You need an unshaded lamp with a single bulb across the room from a blank section of wall. The curtains or blinds should be closed. Hold your hands a metre or so from the wall and adjust them until the shadow looks sharp. The further you move from the wall, the larger and fuzzier the shadow will be.

Making Hand Shadows

My father taught me to make an eagle, a swan and a dog:

- **Eagle**   Cross your hands at the wrists, with your palms facing towards you. Lock your thumbs to form the eagle's head and neck. Curve the other fingers to make wings, which you can gracefully flap to make the eagle move.
- **Swan**   Bend your left arm at the elbow. Bend your left hand at the wrist and the base of the fingers, holding the thumb straight across, to form the swan's head and beak. Hold your right hand along the top of your left arm, spreading out the thumb and four fingers to make the swan's tail feathers.
- **Dog**   Press both palms together, keeping the first three fingers of both hands together and moving the two little fingers back towards your arm together — this makes the dog's mouth, which you can open and shut. To make the ears, separate your thumbs.

Here are some more arty-crafty things to do with paint and paper and wool and other bits and pieces.

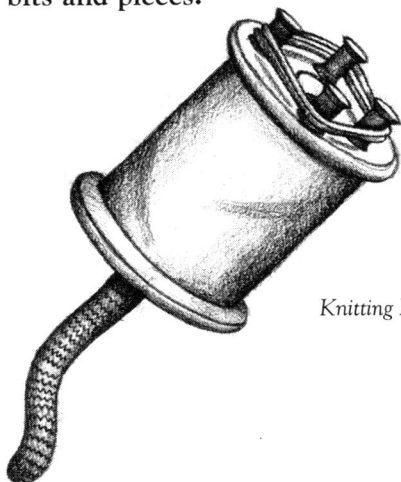

Knitting Nancy

Knitting Nancy

INGREDIENTS
**4 bulletin-board push pins (the kind with long cylindrical heads)
large wooden cotton reel
fine yarn**
EQUIPMENT
**tack hammer
pencil, crochet hook or knitting needle**

Tack the push pins into one end of the cotton reel, setting them at an equal distance from each other.

To start knitting, drop the end of a length of fine yarn down the middle of the cotton reel. Going anti-clockwise around the top of the Knitting Nancy, wind the yarn once around each push-pin head until you are back where you started. Now, begin again at the head where you started and wind the yarn once around again.

Then, using the pencil, crochet hook or knitting needle, lift the bottom loop up and over the yarn. Continue winding and lifting around the push-pin heads in the same way. Each time you finish one round, give a gentle tug to the end protruding from the bottom of the cotton reel so that the knitting comes out evenly.

Weave-a-wheel

If you can find an old bicycle wheel or scooter wheel, try making it into a woven sculpture by weaving in and out of the spokes with string, raffia or wool in a pattern.

Foot Painting

Everyone knows about finger painting, but foot painting is much messier and funnier. Only for outdoors!

INGREDIENTS
large sheets of butcher's paper or computer paper
tempera paints
EQUIPMENT
masking tape
2 or 3 flat-bottomed paint containers
bowl of soap and water
towel

Spread paper on the ground, using masking tape to secure it in place. Put paints into the paint containers. Sit in a small chair and dip your feet into each of the paints, then paint the paper with them.

Wash your feet with soap and water before going inside!

Web Painting

Spider webs are very beautiful and so complicated. It's extraordinary to think that the spider does all that work in just one night. If you find a web, use it to make a web print.

To do this, you need a can of spray paint and several pieces of paper. Get a friend to stand behind the web and hold up some newspaper so that the spray paint does not go on the other plants or shrubs nearby, or on either of you.

Now, spray the web evenly so that there are droplets of paint all over it, and very gently hold up the piece of white drawing paper, pressing it lightly and evenly against the web. Don't pat the paper or smudge it in any way — just lift the paper away, and you will have a delicate tracing of one of Nature's loveliest works of art.

Fan

INGREDIENTS
sheet of A4 paper
poster paints
EQUIPMENT
medicine dropper
stapler

Fold the paper concertina-style, in folds approximately 2cm (¾in) deep. Open out the folds and drip in a few drops of paint along each fold. Use different colours and patterns to create an interesting effect. Fold again and press to spread the paint, then open out to dry.

To use, bring the folds together on one side and staple shut about 10cm (4in) deep; this makes a 'handle'. Open out the painted folds.

How better to disguise yourself than by wearing a mask? Once you get the idea, you will probably be able to think up lots more ways of making masks or wigs.

Egg Carton Head

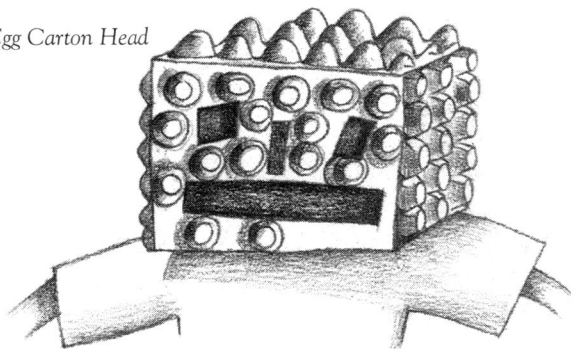

INGREDIENTS
small square cardboard box, to fit over your head
4 cardboard egg cartons
craft glue
poster paints
feathers, straw or bits of string
EQUIPMENT
scissors
paintbrush

Cut the flaps off the box so that it fits neatly over your head. Cut out holes for the eyes, nose and mouth. Open out the egg cartons and, using the cup sections, glue them all over the four sides of the box and on the top. Paint the box with crazy colours and decorate with feathers, straws or bits of string.

Egg Carton Head

Easy Spider Mask

INGREDIENTS
**piece of elastic, 2.5cm (1in) wide and
long enough to fit around your head
8 black pipe-cleaners
small piece of cardboard
acrylic paints or felt-tip pens**

EQUIPMENT
**stapler
scissors
paintbrush**

Ask an adult to staple or stitch the ends of the elastic together to fit snugly around your head. Bend one end of each of the pipe-cleaners to hook in and around the elastic, four to a side. Bend them twice again to make them look like spider legs. Cut out two circles from the cardboard and draw eyes on them, then staple them in place at the front.

Paper Plate Lion Mask

INGREDIENTS
**white paper plate
yellow pencil
poster or acrylic paints, or felt-tip pens
yellow crepe paper or yarn
sticky tape
ice-block stick**

EQUIPMENT
**scissors
paintbrush
stapler**

Colour or paint the paper plate yellow. Draw on a lion's face with the felt-tip pens.

Cut strips of yellow crepe paper or yarn and glue or staple them around the top of the face to form a mane. Tape an ice-block stick to the bottom of the back as a handle.

Wool Wig

Would you like to have long yellow plaits? Or orange curls with purple bows? Or long, long green or pink hair?

INGREDIENTS
**3–4 skeins of wool or rug yarn, cut into
60cm (2ft) lengths for a short wig, or
90cm (3ft) lengths for a medium one, or
120cm (4ft) lengths for a really long one
2–3 lengths of string, the length of the
front of your hairline to the
nape of your neck**

EQUIPMENT
scissors

Divide all the wool or rug yarn into bunches of three strands. Place the lengths of string flat on a table or the floor, and tie the ends to the middle of one bunch of wool. Continue to tie bunches of wool to the centre strings — this is the 'part' — pressing them closely together.

Put the wig on your head and style in the way you want — plaits or a ponytail, for instance. Trim the ends to make them even.

Years ago, when I was studying Ancient History at school, I found it fascinating to learn that many toys and games that children still play with today were ancient in origin — tops, for instance, and hoops, or the Aeolian Harp project described here. Some ideas and projects, like the Three-Legged Stool, the Boomerang and Wishbones, are probably as old as humanity itself.

Aeolian Harp

Many centuries ago the Greeks made beautifully carved musical instruments called Aeolian harps. They placed them in the windows and doorways of their homes and temples, where they caught the breeze and played gentle, magical music.

INGREDIENTS
2 pieces of pine board, each 6mm (¼in) thick, 12.5cm (5in) wide and 35cm (14in) long
2 pieces of the same thickness of pine board, each 5cm (2in) wide and 12.5cm (5in) long
nails
12 large eyelet screws
2 short pieces of dowelling, each approx. 2cm (¾in) thick and 12.5cm (5in) long
set of 6 guitar strings (from music shop)

EQUIPMENT
hammer
pencil
drill

Aeolian Harp

Nail the two short end pieces of pine board to one of the long pieces of pine board; turn over.

Use the pencil to mark two lines about 5cm (2in) from the short ends, and either mark six places on each for the eyelet screws or, if the pine board is very hard, use a drill bit to make it easier. Screw in the eyelet screws.

About another 5cm in from the eyelet screws, nail down the two pieces of dowelling. Knot the six guitar strings between the six sets of eyelet screws, in descending order of thickness.

Tune the strings by tightening first one set of eyelet screws, starting with the thinnest string, and turning it until the string makes a low strumming sound when you pluck it. Tighten all the other sets of strings until they make the same low note when plucked — the thick strings will have to be tightened much further than the thin ones.

Place the second long piece of pine board on top of the box and nail down lightly to secure.

Put the harp on an open windowsill where the breeze will pass through in varying strengths to 'play' it.

Three-Legged Stool

Native Americans used to make these stools, and so did the tribes of Africa. The idea still works well today. Try it out next time you go camping or walking.

EQUIPMENT
**3 sturdy thick short sticks, each about
60cm (2ft) long rope**

Hold the three sticks together loosely in the middle. Wrap the rope loosely around the middle two or three times and knot it (make sure this is loose, not tight).

Spread two of the sticks to form an X-shape. Move the third stick to rest in the fork of the other two, at an even distance from them both, so that the three form a sort of pocket, top and bottom.

Test to see if you can sit in the stool by propping each side of your bottom on two of the sticks and putting the third one at your back. If the sticks are evenly balanced, they should spread out to take your weight evenly. You may have to experiment a few times but it is worth it, being far more comfortable than squatting or sitting on wet ground.

Water Divining

In ancient times, tribes would call on the services of a
special water diviner to help them find clean water for their
camp. These people were able to tell where the water was
underground by a special tingling feeling up their arms.
Sometimes they just sensed its presence.
Farmers still often use water diviners
to help them find water bores or an underground stream
that they can tap.

Maybe you have a 'feeling' for water (some people say that if your star sign is a 'water' one, like Aquarius, it is a gift you may have been born with). The most usual tool for divining water is a forked stick, but some diviners even use a fork of wire.

Walk around with the forked stick in front of you and see if you can feel any different signals coming through (imagine you are like a TV station, and 'tune in' to the waves). If your hands tingle, maybe there is an underground drain, river or stormwater channel nearby.

Boomerang

The returning boomerang was used by Australian Aborigines for many centuries. When thrown correctly through the air, the boomerang will return, in a perfect arc, to the person who threw it.

INGREDIENTS
medium-weight cardboard
EQUIPMENT
pencil
ruler
scissors

Sketch the boomerang shape onto the cardboard. Cut it out carefully. Do not bend or buckle the cardboard as this will affect the boomerang's ability to fly.

To throw, hold your left hand, palm-side down, at eye level. Rest the boomerang on your left hand so that one leg extends past your fingers, balanced. Use the index finger of your right hand to strike the extended leg sharply so that the boomerang shoots off straight outwards, not down. You will probably have to practise to get it just right.

Wishbones

Keep the wishbone when you have chicken for dinner. Wash it and dry it and put it in the fridge, hanging it over one of the rungs so that it becomes cold and dry.

One player hooks their little finger around the bottom of one end (not too high up the shaft — that's cheating!) and the other person does the same. To win a wish, pull the wishbone straight apart. Whoever gets the piece with the tab on top gets the wish. Oh, and don't tell anyone your wish, or it won't come true.

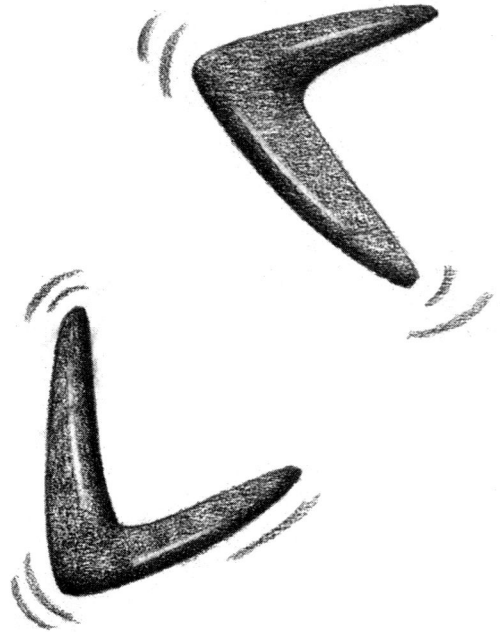

INDEX